CHICKEN BREASTS

CHICKEN BREASTS

116 new and classic recipes for the fairest part of the fowl

BY DIANE ROZAS

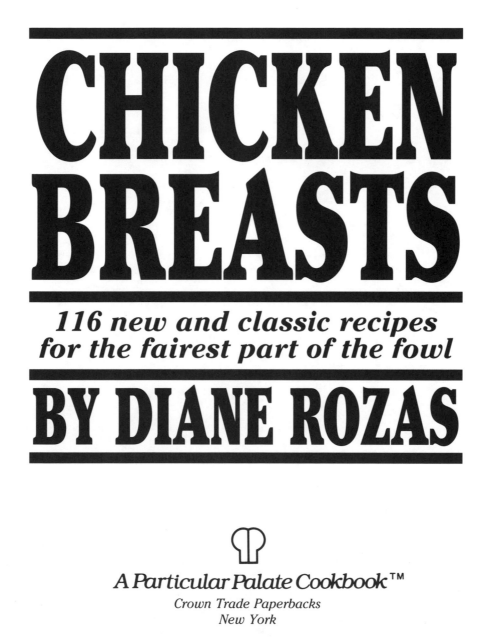

A Particular Palate Cookbook™

Crown Trade Paperbacks
New York

To my darling parents, Helen and Felix

A Particular Palate Cookbook

Copyright © 1985, 1996 by Diane Rozas

Published by Crown Trade Paperbacks, 201 East 50th Street, New York, New York 10022. Member of the Crown Publishing Group.

Originally published by Harmony Books, a division of Crown Publishers, Inc. in 1985

Random House, Inc. New York, Toronto, London, Sydney, Auckland

CROWN TRADE PAPERBACKS, PARTICULAR PALATE, and colophons are trademarks of Crown Publishers, Inc.

Printed in The United States of America

Library of Congress Cataloging-in-Publication Data

Rozas, Diane.

   Chicken breasts.
   "A Particular palate cookbook."— Includes index.
   1. Cookery (Chicken)   I. Title.
   TX750.R69   1984
   641.6'65   85-780
              CIP

ISBN 0-517-88705-2

10 9 8 7 6 5 4 3 2 1

Second Edition

Contents

Introduction

" . . . poultry is for the cook what canvas is for the painter."

BRILLAT-SAVARIN

Over the past few years, chicken breasts have become a culinary phenomenon. More and more frequently, they appear on the dinner table at home, on restaurant menus, in picnic baskets, on barbecue grills, and even at fast-food chains across the country. What's more, chicken breasts have become as popular as many traditional main dishes, such as beef, shrimp, and veal.

Why this sudden surge of acceptance? Chicken breasts are affordable. They're healthy—low in calories and animal fats, high in protein. They're tender, delightfully flavored, and, above all, incredibly versatile, lending themselves to almost every style of cooking, from nouvelle to northern Chinese. And because chicken breasts marry magnificently with so many different ingredients, it's safe to say they have become a "cuisine" unto themselves.

No doubt you're aware of these virtues, but you may find yourself preparing chicken breasts in the same old way, which can make anything seem boring. *Chicken Breasts* contains more than 100 delectable ways out of the dilemma, with recipes for entrees and appetizers, to please a crowd or just two, and for serving chicken breasts in every shape and form—whole, halved, on the bone and off. Included are sumptuous sautés, Oriental-style stir-fry recipes, an inspired array of grilling and broiling marinades, basting sauces and flavored butters, along with tasty contributions from accomplished chefs and restaurateurs.

There are recipes for chicken breasts sauced in a simple tarragon cream, stuffed with chicken liver pâté, shaped into dainty paupiettes, and deep-fried with hazelnuts. Recipes for the tenderest poaches, surprising salads, spicy enchiladas, rellenos, Bastille, pot pie, and more. You'll also find lots of suggestions for buying, boning, and storing the delicate white meat, as well as interesting tidbits of information on cooking, serving, and eating the amazingly popular chicken breast.

Dressed up or down, served simply or elaborately, chicken breasts satisfy the palate and the pocketbook. And when it comes to serving chicken breasts with flair and flavor, these recipes will deliciously provide the dash of inspiration you've been seeking.

Preparing Chicken Breasts

These few simple suggestions may be worth some extra money in your pocket and the tenderest, tastiest dishes for your cooking efforts.

Skinning and boning the chicken breasts yourself can save you as much as several dollars per pound. Also, the chicken breasts will remain moister, fresher, and more succulent when prepared just before cooking. That's because the bone and skin act as a natural encasement, preventing the delicate meat from drying out—the greatest detriment to its final flavor and texture. It's a simple process, taking only a few minutes once you've had a little practice. The process can be made even easier if you put the chicken breast in the freezer for a half hour before you begin. Don't forget to save the bones to make a large pot of homemade stock (see page 11). What to do with the "other" parts? If, by chance, a chicken thigh or leg finds its way into a recipe, certainly the dish will survive. If so, don't forget, the dark meat takes longer to cook, especially on the grill or in the broiler.

BUYING CHICKEN BREASTS Look for large, plump breasts, free of bruises. Pick only those with a well-rounded breast and a flexible backbone. Use your nose to determine absolute freshness—it should have no odor whatsoever. Color is not a factor in flavor, just a reflection of the different chicken feeds used from region to region throughout the country.

CHICKEN BREASTS

Technically, a whole chicken breast consists of two attached halves (before it is split). When split, the two halves are called chicken breasts. When skinned, boned, and halved, they are called suprêmes or, even chicken cutlets. In many cases skinning is optional, especially when grilling or barbecuing, and depends totally on your taste.

Weight: A whole chicken breast weighs between 13 and 16 ounces before the skin and bone are removed.

Serving Size: One half of a plump chicken breast—6½ ounces—is a perfect average serving size. If the suprêmes (or cutlets) weigh less, figure on serving two per person, especially to those with large appetites.

Calories: In the average 6½-ounce serving, there are only 197 slim calories. That's all!

SKINNING AND BONING A WHOLE CHICKEN BREAST

1. Place the whole breast on a work surface, skin side up. Peel the skin back and off. Trim away any remaining bits of skin and fat.

2. Using a very sharp boning knife with a flexible blade (see page 12), insert the tip at one end of the rib, between the cage and the meat. Keeping the knife as close as possible to the rib cage, work it along the edge of the breast from one end to the other.

3. Separate the meat from the bone to a depth of 2 inches. (At this point the breast meat will still be attached in the center to the breastbone, on both sides.)

4. With the knife and your fingers, scrape or push the meat toward the breastbone until it is *completely* loosened from the rib cage but still attached to the breastbone.

5. With the point of the knife, work around the wishbone; loosen and remove.

6. Now scrape and push the meat away from the breastbone, being careful not to tear the meat. Remove the breast meat.

SPLITTING A CHICKEN BREAST AND REMOVING THE TENDON

1. Using your sharp boning knife, slice the breast in half following the center indentation where it was attached to the bone.

2. Slip the point of the boning knife under one end of the white tendon running along the underside of the breast and lift the tendon away from the meat, holding an end of the tendon with one hand while lifting and scraping the meat carefully away.

FLATTENING CHICKEN BREASTS Flatten chicken breasts to a uniform thickness with a flat-headed metal pounder or wooden mallet. Place the breasts between sheets of waxed paper or plastic wrap, skin side up, and pound with light, even strokes to the required thinness.

STORING CHICKEN BREASTS At this point, if you are not cooking the prepared breasts immediately, wrap them tightly in individual plastic sandwich bags or several layers of plastic wrap to keep them from drying out, and refrigerate or freeze until needed.

A FEW WORDS ABOUT INGREDIENTS

Bread Crumbs: Bread crumbs are either fresh or dry. For fresh bread crumbs, put 2 to 3 slices of bread in a blender or food processor at one time, and process until fine. For dry, leave bread out to dry before crumbing. Store dried bread crumbs in an airtight container.

Butter, Clarified Butter, and Oil: When butter is called for, use unsalted (sweet) butter; you can always add salt to the recipe in the proper proportion.

Clarified butter is butter with the milk solids removed. To make clarified butter, cut sweet butter into small pieces into a saucepan. Melt the butter over low heat and skim off the foam. Take the pan off the heat and let it stand for a few minutes. When the butter is clear, pour it through a layer of cheesecloth into a container. Discard the residue. Store the clarified butter in the refrigerator for up to two months.

Oils can be either virgin olive oil or vegetable oils such as safflower, corn, peanut, and, in a few cases, sesame oil (use only in Oriental-style stir-fry recipes, not to be confused with the sesame seed oil sold in health food stores). Oils should always be fresh, never previously used for frying.

Chicken Stock: To prepare stock, into a heavy saucepan put 1 pound chicken parts, including back, neck, wings, and bones, along with 1 chopped carrot, 1 sliced onion, 1 celery stalk, 1 poaching bouquet (optional; see below). Add 10 black peppercorns, 5 whole cloves, 5 sprigs of parsley, and a large bay leaf. Cover the ingredients with 3 to 4 cups water and bring to a rapid boil. With a spoon, remove any foamy scum that collects on top of the water; reduce the heat and simmer, uncovered, for 1 hour. Strain and store in a glass jar in the refrigerator, or freeze in a plastic container. For small amounts, freeze stock in ice cube trays and then put the stock cubes in plastic freezer bags. Frozen, stock will last for up to 3 months; refrigerated, for 3 days.

Cream, Sour Cream, and Crème Fraîche: When cream is called for, use heavy, or whipping, cream unless otherwise specified. Sour cream should be the dairy variety; imitation does not have the delicate richness of the real thing, and it separates if heated.

Crème fraîche, or French cultured cream, can be easily made with 2½ cups heavy cream and 2 tablespoons of buttermilk, mixed together and left to stand for 3 to 4 hours in a warm (75° to 80° F.) area near or on the stove.

Herbs, Spices, and Flavorings: Use fresh herbs whenever they are available. If not, make sure the dried herbs you have are aromatic and have been stored in airtight containers, away from heat and light. Black pepper should always be ground at the moment of use, as its flavor dissipates quickly. Many of these recipes require flavorful combinations of herbs and spices in partnership with butter, wine, cream, and other ingredients to enhance the flavors. Herbs and spices are also used before cooking in marinades to infuse the delicate white meat with delicious bursts of both common and exotic richness. Herbs and spices should always be of top quality and as fresh as possible.

Marinades: There are two types of marinades, wet and dry. Wet marinades include enough liquid to partially immerse chicken breasts before cooking and later are also used as basting sauces. Dry marinades usually include a combination of herbs and spices and perhaps a small amount of oil, which is rubbed into the chicken. After combining the marinade ingredients with the chicken breast, allow enough time for the flavors to penetrate. Luckily, chicken breasts absorb flavors quickly: 1 to 4 hours at room temperature. Some wet marinades, such as those with lemon juice or wine, also act as tenderizers. Liqueurs impart strong flavors, so use them sparingly.

Poaching Bouquets: Perhaps the most popular and the best-known is the classic French bouquet garni, which always includes a bay leaf, fresh parsley, and thyme. Other ingredients can be added to a poaching bouquet, such as a stalk of celery or celery tops, leek greens, a fennel bulb, and garlic. Poaching bouquets can either be tied in a bundle with kitchen string or tied in a cheesecloth bag, which is a good idea for such ingredients as garlic, cloves, peppercorns, and lemon zest.

Wines and Liqueurs: Wine imparts a wonderful nutty flavor as the alcohol evaporates in the cooking process. Almost any wine or liqueur can be used in cooking chicken breasts—vermouth, red or white table wines, Madeira, Marsala, brandy, Cognac, etc.; experimentation is highly recommended. When wine or liquor is added to ingredients, the alcohol must be burned off—either by flaming or by rapidly cooking—in order for the raw quality to evaporate, leaving behind only the essence of that ingredient.

A FEW WORDS ABOUT EQUIPMENT

Barbecue Grill: A chicken breast cooked over burning embers is certainly a tasty treat. Whether a small hibachi or a gas-burning barbecue is used, the tender meat will cook quickly. Marinate before cooking to ensure a flavorful taste throughout.

Basting Brush: For grilling or broiling, a long-handled brush will help distribute a sauce or marinade over the meat's surface.

Boning Knife: A stainless-steel-coated blade made of high-carbon steel is best. The blade, 5 to 5½ inches (with a total length of about 11 inches, including the handle), should be flexible.

Mallet: A flat-edged mallet, a pounding bat, or a rolling pin is recommended for flattening chicken breasts.

Pepper Mill: Pepper is one of the essentials for flavorful, properly seasoned chicken breasts. The flavor of pepper subsides almost immediately after it is ground, so the pre-ground pepper in a little can on your spice shelf doesn't do much in terms of flavoring food. All pepper mills work on the same principle, so it is not necessary to invest a fortune in an imported precision-made model.

Sauté Pan, Saucepan, and Baking Pans: Many of the quick and easy recipes for chicken breasts start with a simple sauté. The proper pan has a flat bottom and sides that go straight up (unlike a frying pan, which has slanted or slightly rounded sides), and should be made of heavy-gauge and highly conductive metal that transmits heat evenly and steadily without "hot spots." The best material for a sauté pan is copper lined with tin; also acceptable is heavy-gauge aluminum, coated with stainless steel on the inside. A good, strong handle, one that is made separately from the pan, then bolted on, is recommended. The pan should have a tight-fitting lid.

Almost any saucepan can be used when one is called for, and baking dishes can be made of any ovenproof material.

Wok: A bowl-shaped carbon steel Chinese pan used for the stir-fry method of cooking, the wok must be placed on a metal ring stand that fits over the burner of the stove to hold the wok in place. A large frying pan or heavy skillet can be used in place of a wok so long as the fire is high and a tossing motion is used to keep the food in the pan moving and cooking quickly.

Sautéing

Sautéing chicken breasts is one of the simplest ways to bring out their natural succulence and tenderness, provided they are not overcooked. What's more, sautéing is quick—it takes no more than 10 minutes to prepare a recipe from beginning to end.

Sautéing requires a sauté pan or heavy skillet, and a minimum of fat or oil. The chicken breasts are cooked rapidly over high heat, so that the meat turns a beautiful and appetizing golden brown outside yet remains moist and tender inside.

Once mastered, the sauté method of cooking chicken breasts can open a whole new world of inventive cookery for you. These simple sautés can be made snappier with a splash of vermouth, stronger with shallots or garlic, more colorful with a slightly sautéed tomato, or richer with a dollop of crème fraîche. Many of these sauté recipes will make light of your work and get you out of the kitchen quickly, without ever cheating the palate of its just deserts, and at the same time offering a perfect opportunity to be creative.

CHICKEN BREASTS with SAGE AND RED WINE

2–4 servings

4 tablespoons (½ stick) butter (page 10)
2 whole chicken breasts (about 2 pounds),
    boned and halved
4 fresh sage leaves (or ½ teaspoon crumbled
    dried sage)
Salt and black pepper to taste
½ cup dry red wine
¼ cup chicken stock

1. In a sauté pan or heavy skillet over medium-high heat, melt the clarified butter; add the chicken breasts and sauté for 2 to 3 minutes on each side, or just lightly browned.

2. Lower the heat to medium and add the sage. Sprinkle on the salt and pepper; stir in ¼ cup of the red wine. Cook, covered, for 8 minutes; uncover the pan and cook for 2 minutes more, or until chicken breasts are tender. Remove to a heated platter and keep warm.

3. To the pan add the remaining ¼ cup of wine and the stock. Turn up the heat and boil until reduced by half. Pour the sauce over the chicken.

CHICKEN BREASTS WITH TARRAGON AND WHITE WINE

In step 2, add 2 tablespoons olive oil to the pan; add ½ cup chopped shallots and cook 5 minutes, or until tender. Substitute 4 tablespoons chopped fresh tarragon leaves (or 1 tablespoon dried) for the sage and white wine for the red. Continue as directed.

A WORD ABOUT HERBS

Fresh or dried? Which should you use?

Since the availability of fresh herbs in your market can be subject to seasonal comings and goings, and because most of us no longer have the lovingly tended, highly prized herb gardens of our pastoral heritage, we are sometimes forced to turn to little bottles, cans, and cellophane packages of the aromatic substances in order to enhance the flavor of our foods. Of course, fresh herbs are always better. But cooking with dried is not as sinful a substitution as using a bouillon cube in place of homemade stock. Dried herbs can be successfully incorporated into your recipes by following this simple suggestion: Unless the dried herbs are going to be cooked for at least 30 minutes with liquid ingredients, pour boiling water over them through a small strainer. Squeeze out the water before adding the herbs to other ingredients. This step refreshes the herbs and brings them back to life—to a state more closely resembling fresh.

There are a few simple rules to follow regarding herbs, spices, and flavorings. Never, never, never use dried parsley; in flavor and texture it closely resembles sawdust. The same goes for preground black pepper (always use freshly ground from a pepper mill), seasoned salt, onion powder, garlic powder, and plain white vinegar, which should be used only to clean the bottoms of copper pots.

CHICKEN BREASTS PERNOD

3–6 servings

Pernod, a semisweet anise or licorice-flavored liqueur, is often drunk as an aperitif in France. Cooked with chicken breasts, it makes for a most interesting flavor combination.

8 tablespoons (1 stick) butter
4 carrots, minced
½ tart green apple, peeled and minced
1 small yellow onion, minced
½ celery stalk, minced
1½ cups chicken stock
1 bouquet garni (see page 11), tied in a
    cheesecloth bag
½ teaspoon salt
Black pepper to taste
½ cup heavy cream
3 whole chicken breasts (about 3 pounds),
    skinned, boned, and halved
3 garlic cloves, finely minced
2 tablespoons Pernod
Chopped fresh chives for garnish

1. To prepare the sauce, in a sauté pan over medium heat melt 3 tablespoons of the butter. Add the carrots, apple, onion, and celery; sauté gently for about 5 minutes; do not brown. Add ½ cup of chicken stock, the bouquet garni, salt, and pepper. Simmer for about 15 minutes, or until the vegetables are very soft.

2. Squeeze the liquid from the cheesecloth bag and throw the bag away. Put the sautéed vegetables in a blender or food processor fitted with the steel blade and purée. Add the cream and blend thoroughly.

3. In a sauté pan or heavy skillet over medium-high heat, melt 4 tablespoons of the butter. Sauté the chicken breasts for 2 to 3 minutes on each side, or just until lightly browned. Add the garlic, cover, and cook over medium heat for about 5 minutes, or until tender. Transfer the chicken breasts to a heated platter and keep warm.

4. Remove any excess fat from the pan. Turn the heat to medium-high, pour in the Pernod, and cook, scraping up any brown bits from the sides and bottom of the pan.

5. Add the remaining stock and continue cooking until the liquid is reduced by half. Reduce the heat to low, add the vegetable purée, and cook for about 5 minutes. Stir the remaining 1 tablespoon of butter into the sauce, put the chicken breast pieces on individual serving plates, and spoon on the sauce.

NORMANDY-STYLE CHICKEN BREASTS

Fresh apple and Calvados, apple brandy from Normandy, are the ingredients in this classic recipe.

2–4 servings

5 tablespoons clarified butter (page 10)
2 whole chicken breasts (about 2 pounds), skinned, boned, and halved
2 tablespoons minced shallots
1 tart green apple, peeled, cored, and finely chopped
¾ cup Calvados
¾ cup chicken stock
½ cup heavy cream
2 tart green apples, peeled, cored, and cut into ¼-inch rounds
Salt and white pepper to taste

1. In a sauté pan or heavy skillet over medium-high heat, melt the butter. Add the chicken breasts and sauté for 2 to 3 minutes on each side, or until lightly browned. Do not overcook. Remove the chicken breasts to a heated platter and set aside.

2. In the same pan, sauté the shallots and chopped apple until browned. Reduce the heat. Add the Calvados and ½ cup of the chicken stock; bring to a simmer and return the chicken breasts to the pan. Cover and cook for 8 to 10 minutes more.

3. Remove the chicken breasts to a heated platter, leaving the juices in the pan; keep warm. Add the cream, the remaining ¼ cup chicken stock, and the apple rounds to the pan. Simmer for about 5 minutes, until the apples are tender and the sauce has thickened. Season with salt and pepper.

4. Arrange the chicken breasts and apple rounds on individual plates and pour equal amounts of sauce over each.

CHICKEN BREAST WITH COINTREAU In step 2, sauté 1 minced garlic clove with the shallots and chopped apple. Substitute 4 tablespoons Cointreau for the Calvados.

CHICKEN BREASTS PAPRIKA

2–4 servings

2 whole chicken breasts (about 2 pounds), skinned, boned, and flattened slightly
Salt and black pepper
1½ tablespoons Hungarian paprika (sweet or mild)

3 tablespoons butter
¼ cup finely chopped onion
½ cup dry white wine
½ cup chicken stock
¾ cup sour cream
Finely chopped parsley for garnish

1. Sprinkle the chicken breasts with salt and pepper and paprika.

2. Melt the butter in a sauté pan or heavy skillet over medium-high heat. Sauté the chicken breasts for 2 to 3 minutes on each side, or until lightly browned. Remove the chicken breasts to a heated platter and set aside.

3. Add the onion to the pan and sauté over medium heat until translucent. Turn the heat up to medium-high and add the wine, stirring to dissolve any brown particles remaining on the bottom of the pan. Continue cooking until the liquid is reduced by half. Return the chicken breasts to the pan, add the stock, and simmer for 4 to 5 minutes, or until the chicken breasts are tender.

4. Remove the chicken breasts from the pan and place on a heated platter. Over a very low fire, stir in the sour cream and heat the sauce through, for about 1 minute or less. Spoon the sauce over the chicken breasts and sprinkle with parsley.

SALTIMBOCCA

2–4 servings

A twist on an Italian classic usually made with veal. *Saltimbocca* means "jumps in your mouth."

4 fresh whole sage leaves (or ½ teaspoon finely crumbled dried leaves)
2 whole chicken breasts, boned, skinned, and flattened to ¼ inch, and trimmed to about 5 inches square
¼ pound thinly sliced prosciutto
3 tablespoons butter
Salt and black pepper to taste
3 tablespoons dry white wine

1. Divide sage evenly or sprinkle a quarter of the dried sage over each piece of chicken breast. Top each with a slice of prosciutto. Secure together with a toothpick (which will be removed after sautéing).

2. In a sauté pan or heavy skillet over medium-high heat, melt the butter. Sauté the chicken breasts, starting with the prosciutto side down, for 2 to 3 minutes on each side. Do not overcook. Season with salt and pepper while cooking. Remove the chicken pieces to a heated platter, prosciutto side up, and keep warm.

3. Add the wine to the pan and bring to a boil, stir well, and pour the sauce over the chicken breasts.

MOZZARELLA SALTIMBOCCA Between two chicken breast pieces put a slice of prosciutto and a slice of mozzarella cheese. Sprinkle with the sage and fasten tightly with several toothpicks. Continue with step 2 as directed.

BRANDIED CHICKEN BREASTS

3–6 servings

8 tablespoons (1 stick) butter
3 whole chicken breasts (about 3 pounds),
    skinned and boned
1 medium onion, finely chopped
Salt and black pepper to taste
1 cup chicken stock
1 cup heavy cream
3 egg yolks
3 tablespoons brandy

1. In a sauté pan or heavy skillet over medium-high heat, melt the butter. Sauté the chicken breasts for 2 to 3 minutes on each side, or just until lightly browned. Add the onion, salt and pepper, and stock. Lower the heat, cover, and simmer for 8 to 10 minutes, or until the chicken breasts are tender. Remove to a heated platter and keep warm.

2. In a bowl, whisk the cream into the egg yolks until well blended; stir in the brandy.

3. With the pan off the heat, stir in the cream mixture. Over a *very* low fire, cook the sauce *just* until it begins to thicken. Do not boil or overcook.

4. Return the chicken breasts to the pan and heat through.

MARSALA CHICKEN BREASTS Omit step 2 and the cream, egg yolks and brandy. Add 3 tablespoons marsala wine to step 3 in place of the cream mixture.

CHICKEN BREASTS with FRESH CHIVES

2–4 servings

2 whole chicken breasts (about 2 pounds),
    skinned, boned, and halved
Salt and white pepper to taste
All-purpose flour for dredging
6 tablespoons (¾ stick) butter
1 cup white port wine or dry vermouth
1¼ cups heavy cream
Juice of ½ lemon
7 tablespoons chopped fresh chives

1. Sprinkle the chicken breasts with salt and pepper. Dredge in the flour; shake off the excess.

2. In a sauté pan or heavy skillet over medium-high heat, melt 3 tablespoons of the butter. Sauté the chicken breasts for 3 to 5 minutes on each side, or until lightly browned. Remove the chicken breasts to a heated platter and set aside.

3. Remove any excess fat remaining in the pan. Add the wine and boil until the liquid is reduced by half. Turn the heat down to low and whisk in the cream until well blended. Whisk in the remaining 3 tablespoons of butter, one at a time, the lemon juice, and 5 tablespoons of the chives. Simmer the sauce for 15 minutes more.

4. Return the chicken breasts to the pan to heat through. Transfer to a heated serving platter, spoon on the sauce, and garnish with the remaining 2 tablespoons chives.

CHICKEN PICCATA

Chicken Piccata is every bit as tasty as veal piccata, and about $10 cheaper per pound. Wild rice is the perfect accompaniment.

2–4 servings

2 whole chicken breasts, skinned, boned, and
     flattened to ¼ inch thick
Salt and black pepper to taste
All-purpose flour for dredging
3 tablespoons butter
1 tablespoon olive oil
2 garlic cloves, peeled and minced
½ pound mushrooms, washed, stemmed,
     and thinly sliced
2 teaspoons fresh lemon juice
½ cup dry white wine
2 teaspoons capers (water-packed), drained
3 tablespoons minced parsley
½ thinly sliced lemon

1. Sprinkle the chicken breasts with salt and pepper. Dredge them in flour and shake off the excess.

2. In a sauté pan or heavy skillet over medium-high heat, melt the butter with the olive oil. Add the garlic and sauté briefly. Add the chicken breasts and sauté for 1 to 2 minutes on each side, or just until lightly browned. Remove to a dish and set aside.

3. Add the mushrooms to the pan and sauté over medium heat for about 1 minute. Return the chicken to the pan; stir in the lemon juice and wine and simmer, covered, for 10 minutes, or until the chicken is tender.

4. Add the capers and heat through. Put the chicken breasts on a platter, spoon on the juices, and garnish with parsley and lemon slices.

HOW HOT IS A HEATED PLATTER?

Serving plates and platters should be heated before cooked food is put on them.

To heat a platter, turn the oven to the lowest setting. Set the platter (or individual dinner plates) on a rack in the center of the oven. If the platter becomes too hot to handle, allow it to cool on the counter before putting the chicken breasts on it; otherwise, the food will continue to cook rather than just keep warm. Place a foil tent over the chicken breasts to retain the heat while you finish the sauce.

CREOLE CURRY CHICKEN BREASTS

A fresh coconut is required for this recipe; really, nothing else will do. Use an ordinary hammer from the tool chest to crack the coconut after the milk has been removed.

4–6 servings

4 tablespoons (½ stick) butter
1 garlic clove, crushed
1 large onion, sliced into thin rounds
3 whole chicken breasts (about 3 pounds), skinned and halved
1 small red pepper, finely chopped (or ¼ teaspoon crushed red pepper flakes)
2½ tablespoons curry powder
¼ teaspoon ground ginger
Pinch of powdered saffron (or 1 thread, chopped)
Salt to taste
4 tablespoons sugar
¼ cup chicken stock
1 fresh coconut, grated white part (meat) only and milk

1. Melt the butter in a sauté pan or heavy skillet over medium heat. Add the garlic and cook until brown. Add the onion and sauté for 3 minutes more.

2. Increase the heat to medium-high, add the chicken breasts, bone side up, and sauté for 1 to 2 minutes on each side, or until lightly browned. Remove the chicken breasts to a dish and set aside. To the sauté pan add the red pepper, curry powder, ginger, saffron, salt, and sugar. Lower the heat and simmer together for 1 minute.

3. Return the chicken breasts to the pan; add the stock and coconut. Cover and simmer for 20 minutes, or until the chicken breasts are very tender; after the first 10 minutes, add the coconut milk, making sure heat is on low.

CHICKEN BREASTS with PEACHES

For a slightly tart taste, substitute ½ cup white wine or Champagne for half the chicken stock.

2–4 servings

2 cups fresh, ripe peaches (about 4 medium), peeled and sliced
6 tablespoons fresh lemon juice
1 tablespoon sugar
2 whole chicken breasts (about 2 pounds), skinned, boned, and halved
Salt and black pepper to taste
½ teaspoon paprika
2 tablespoons vegetable oil
1 cup chicken stock
4 tablespoons (½ stick) butter
1 cup finely chopped onion

1. Mix together the peaches, lemon juice, and sugar and set aside.

2. Sprinkle the chicken breasts with salt and pepper and paprika. Heat the oil in a sauté pan or heavy skillet over medium-high heat and sauté the breasts for 2 to 3 minutes on each side, or until lightly browned. Add the stock, cover, and simmer for 8 to 10 minutes, or until the chicken breasts are tender. Set aside.

3. In the same pan over medium heat, melt 2 tablespoons of the butter and sauté the onion until golden brown. Remove the onion to a bowl. Drain the juices from the peaches into the onion and set aside.

4. Over medium heat, melt the remaining 2 tablespoons butter in the sauté pan. Add the peaches and sauté until tender. Return the onion mixture and the liquid from the chicken breasts to the pan. Cover and simmer for 10 minutes. Return the chicken breasts to the pan and simmer for 2 minutes more, or just until heated through.

CHERRY CHICKEN Substitute tart Queen Anne cherries for the peaches.

CHICKEN BREASTS with CHAMPAGNE

2–4 servings

5 tablespoons butter
2 whole chicken breasts (about 2 pounds), skinned, boned, and flattened slightly
Salt and black pepper to taste
1 cup chicken stock
1 cup Champagne (Brut or Extra Dry) at room temperature
¼ cup dry white wine
2 tablespoons minced shallots
2 tablespoons Madeira
2 tablespoons minced fresh parsley
1 tablespoon minced fresh tarragon leaves (or ½ teaspoon dried)
2 tablespoons capers (water-packed)

1. In a sauté pan or heavy skillet over medium-high heat, melt 3 tablespoons of the butter. Add the chicken breasts, sprinkle with salt and pepper, and sauté for 2 to 3 minutes on each side. Do not overcook. Remove to a platter and set aside.

2. In a saucepan, combine the stock, Champagne, wine, and shallots. Bring to a boil and cook until the liquid is reduced by half.

3. Lower the heat to medium and stir in the Madeira, parsley, and tarragon. Whisk in the remaining 2 tablespoons of butter, one at a time. When the sauce is slightly thickened, return the chicken breasts to the pan and heat through for about 1 minute. Garnish with capers.

CHICKEN BREASTS FLORENTINE

3–6 servings

6 tablespoons (¾ stick) butter
2 bunches fresh spinach (stems removed
    only), well washed and dried
Salt and black pepper to taste
Juice of ½ lemon
2 tablespoons vegetable oil
3 whole chicken breasts (about 3 pounds),
    skinned and boned
1 cup port wine or golden sherry
½ cup chicken stock
½ cup heavy cream

1. In a heavy skillet over medium heat, melt 1 tablespoon of the butter. Cook the spinach just until wilted. Season with salt and pepper; add the lemon juice and toss gently. Set aside in the pan.

2. In sauté pan or heavy skillet over medium-high heat, melt 1 tablespoon of the butter and the oil together. Sauté the chicken breasts for about 3 to 5 minutes on each side, or just until lightly browned. Remove the chicken breasts to a heated platter and keep warm.

3. Remove any excess fat from the pan. Pour in the wine, bring to a boil, and cook until the liquid is reduced by half. Lower the heat and add the stock and cream; continue cooking until the sauce is slightly thickened. Remove the pan from the heat and whisk in the remaining 4 tablespoons of butter, one tablespoon at a time. Season with salt and pepper and heat through.

4. Reheat the spinach for just a few seconds. Divide the spinach among individual serving plates. Place a chicken breast on each bed of spinach and drizzle the sauce over the top.

"God sends meat, and the devil sends cooks."

English proverb

CHICKEN BREASTS IN PIQUANT CREAM

2–4 servings

2 whole chicken breasts (about 2 pounds),
    skinned, boned, and halved
Salt and black pepper to taste
4 tablespoons (½ stick) butter
4 garlic cloves, peeled and halved
4 tablespoons white wine vinegar
5 tablespoons dry white wine
1 tablespoon Dijon-style mustard
4 tablespoons tomato purée
¼ cup heavy cream
1 teaspoon Worcestershire sauce

1. Sprinkle the chicken breasts with salt and pepper.

2. In a sauté pan or heavy skillet over medium heat, melt the butter. Add the chicken breasts and the garlic and sauté for 2 or 3 minutes on each side, or until the chicken breasts are lightly browned. Pour in the vinegar and wine; continue cooking for 5 to 7 minutes more, or until the liquid has almost totally evaporated. Remove the chicken breasts to a heated platter and keep warm. Discard the garlic.

3. To the pan add the mustard and tomato purée and stir until smooth, using a few drops of wine if necessary. Place the pan over very low heat, stir in the cream and Worcestershire sauce, and whisk until well blended. Heat through and pour over the chicken breasts.

BRAZILIAN CHICKEN BREASTS with SAUTEED BANANAS

Traditionally, Brazilians serve this dish with fried julienne potatoes.

2–4 servings

5 tablespoons butter
2 large bananas, peeled and sliced lengthwise
1 tablespoon vegetable oil
2 whole chicken breasts (about 2 pounds), skinned, boned, and halved
¼ teaspoon ground ginger
Salt and black pepper to taste
3 tablespoons dark rum
⅓ cup dry white wine

1. In a sauté pan or heavy skillet over medium heat, melt 3 tablespoons butter. Sauté the bananas for 4 to 5 minutes, until brown and crispy. Transfer to a heated platter and set aside.

2. Add the remaining 2 tablespoons butter and the oil to the sauté pan; increase the heat to medium-high. Sprinkle the chicken breasts with ginger and salt and pepper; sauté for 3 to 5 minutes on each side. Remove the breasts to a heated platter and keep warm.

3. Turn the heat to very low. Add the rum to the sauté pan, and after it heats through, about 30 seconds, touch a lighted kitchen match to the rum gently and allow the alcohol to burn off, stirring the sauce as the flame subsides. (Be careful to keep your head out of the way, as alcohol flames can shoot up.)

4. Return the chicken breasts to the pan. Add the white wine and cook over medium heat for 3 minutes, or until the sauce begins to thicken.

5. Put the chicken breasts on the platter between the banana slices, and pour on the sauce.

CHICKEN BREASTS with RASPBERRIES

2–4 servings

4 tablespoons (½ stick) butter
2 whole chicken breasts (about 2 pounds),
    boned, skinned, halved, and flattened to
    ⅓ inch thick
Pinch of salt and white pepper
⅓ cup finely chopped onion
⅓ cup raspberry vinegar
⅓ cup chicken stock
¼ cup heavy cream
30 whole fresh raspberries (about ¾ pint)

1. In a sauté pan or a heavy skillet over medium-high heat, melt the butter. Add the chicken breasts and sauté for 2 to 3 minutes on each side, or until lightly browned. Sprinkle with salt and white pepper; remove to a platter and set aside.

2. Add the onion to the pan and sauté over medium-high heat until tender. Add the vinegar and reduce the liquid to one quarter of the original amount, or until syrupy.

3. Reduce the heat and stir in the stock and cream. Simmer for 2 to 3 minutes. Add the chicken breasts and continue cooking for 5 minutes more. Put the chicken pieces on a heated platter; immediately add the raspberries to the sauce and *gently* cook over very low heat for 1 minute. *Do not stir.*

4. Pour the raspberry sauce over the chicken breasts.

CHICKEN BREASTS WITH BLUEBERRIES
Substitute blueberry vinegar for raspberry and fresh blueberries for the raspberries.

CHICKEN BREASTS VERONIQUE

A simple but very popular French recipe that uses seedless green grapes. If you want to go all out, peel the grapes!

2–4 servings

2 whole chicken breasts (about 2 pounds),
    boned, skinned, and halved
Salt and black pepper
2 tablespoons all-purpose flour
4 tablespoons (½ stick) butter
2 cups dry white wine
2 tablespoons fresh lemon juice
2 tablespoons slivered almonds
8 ounces (½ pound) seedless green grapes,
    washed, stems removed, and halved
    lengthwise

1. Rub the chicken breasts with a mixture of salt and pepper and flour.

2. Melt the butter in a sauté pan or heavy skillet over medium-high heat. Add the chicken breasts and sauté for 2 to 3 minutes.

3. Add the wine and lemon juice, lower the heat, and simmer for 8 to 10 minutes, or until the breasts are tender. Add the almonds and grapes for the last minute.

4. Transfer the chicken to individual plates and spoon the sauce and grapes over each serving.

CHICKEN BREASTS MANDARIN Substitute 1 can of mandarin orange segments for the grapes. Reserve ½ cup juice from the oranges and substitute the juice for ½ cup of the white wine. In step 3, add ¼ teaspoon fines herbes.

MEDITERRANEAN CHICKEN BREASTS

3–6 servings

3 whole chicken breasts (3 pounds), skinned
Salt and black pepper to taste
¼ cup olive oil
¾ cup dry white or red wine
2 medium tomatoes, peeled, seeded, and
    coarsely chopped
2 garlic cloves, finely chopped
⅛ teaspoon dried thyme
¼ teaspoon dried marjoram
¼ teaspoon finely crumbled dried bay leaf
3 sprigs of fresh basil (or ½ teaspoon dried)
½ cup pitted black olives (approximately 15)
3 tablespoons minced Italian flat-leaved
    parsley

1. Sprinkle the chicken breasts with salt and pepper.

2. In a large sauté pan or heavy skillet over medium-high heat, sauté the chicken breasts in the olive oil for 2 to 3 minutes on each side. Remove to a dish and set aside.

3. Pour off any oil left in the pan. Turn the heat down to medium and add the wine. Simmer for about 3 minutes, or until the liquid is reduced by a third. Add the tomatoes, garlic, thyme, marjoram, bay leaf, and basil. Simmer for 5 minutes.

4. Return the chicken breasts to the pan, cover, and simmer for 8 to 10 minutes more, or until chicken is tender. Add the olives and heat through. Transfer to a heated serving platter and sprinkle with parsley.

COOKING WITH WINE

Here's a rule of thumb: If you'd put the wine in a glass and drink it, then it can be used for cooking.

So-called cooking wines contain salt, which will upset the balance of a carefully developed recipe. Stick with good wine and your chicken breasts will turn out great. Every time!

CHICKEN BREASTS with SWEET PEPPERS

Use a combination of sweet red and green bell peppers for an especially colorful effect.

4–6 servings

4 sweet peppers (2 red and 2 green)
3 tablespoons butter
3 tablespoons olive oil
3 whole chicken breasts (about 3 pounds), boned
Salt and black pepper to taste
3 garlic cloves, minced
¼ cup finely chopped onion
2 tablespoons chopped fresh parsley

1. Under direct heat, broil the peppers for about 5 minutes, turning frequently. When the skins have blackened, allow to cool slightly, then peel the loosened skin away from the peppers. Remove the seeds and cut into 1- to 1½-inch pieces. Set aside.

2. In a sauté pan or heavy skillet over medium-high heat, melt 2 tablespoons butter and 2 tablespoons olive oil together. Sauté the chicken breasts for 4 to 5 minutes on each side, or until browned. Sprinkle with salt and black pepper. Remove and set aside.

3. Melt the remaining 1 tablespoon each of butter and oil in the skillet over medium heat. Add the garlic and sauté for 1 minute. Add the onion, reduce the heat, and sauté gently until translucent.

4. Add the parsley, sweet peppers, and chicken breasts to the sauté pan. Cover and simmer for 5 minutes more, or until the chicken breasts are tender.

MAKING PRETTY OF PLAIN

The chicken breast has been accused of adding little to the aesthetics of a dinner plate. However, an ounce of imagination can remedy this problem, if you consider it a problem at all.

Interestingly arranged accompaniments, such as a medley of multicolored vegetables, can do much to enhance the look of a simple meal. Try bedding the chicken breast in a crunchy, buttery cabbage studded with caraway seeds, or crown a fan of cold chicken breast with green and red grapes. Try drizzling on deglazed pan juices, or napping the dinner plate with herb-flecked sauces that show off the delicately browned sauté of chicken breast.

The old standards, parsley sprigs and lemon slices, are always acceptable, but there's more to life. There's orange zest, garlic-scented croutons, watercress purée, a sprinkling of freshly chopped herbs, and thinly sliced fruits. The produce department at your grocery store is full of interesting shapes, textures, and designs for garnishing. And they're edible! Many can even be used as accompaniments.

CHICKEN BREASTS with WINE AND MUSTARD

Experiment with any of the dozens or more of French mustards available in the gourmet section of your market, but please do *not* substitute the bright yellow "hot dog" style mustard.

2–4 servings

2 whole chicken breasts (about 2 pounds),
     skinned, boned, and quartered
Salt and black pepper to taste
6 tablespoons (¾ stick) butter
3 shallots, minced
¾ cup dry white or red wine
1 cup heavy cream
¼ cup chicken stock
4 tablespoons grainy mustard (such as
     Moutarde de Meaux or Pommery)

1. Sprinkle the chicken breasts with salt and pepper. In a sauté pan or heavy skillet over medium-high heat, melt 4 tablespoons of the butter. Sauté the chicken breasts for 3 to 5 minutes on each side, or until browned. Do not overcook. Transfer the chicken pieces to a heated platter and keep warm.

2. Remove any excess fat from the pan. Over medium heat sauté the shallots briefly. Add the wine, cream, and stock; bring to a boil, reduce the heat to medium-low and cook until the sauce has thickened.

3. Whisk in the mustard, combining well. Whisk in the remaining 2 tablespoons of butter, one at a time. Return the chicken to the sauce and heat through for another minute.

4. Place the chicken breasts on individual plates, spoon the sauce over each, and top with a twist of the pepper mill.

Note Half a cup of red port may be substituted for the white or red wine. A large tomato, peeled, seeded, chopped, and sautéed slightly may be added to the sauce after the mustard in step 3.

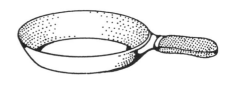

THE SUCCESSFUL SAUTÉ

It is wise to have all the ingredients you will be using measured, chopped, diced, sliced, minced, or melted and within arm's reach before the delicate suprêmes are put into the pan. The extra minute or two it might take to chop parsley or slice a lemon while the chicken breasts are cooking (or overcooking) could mean the difference between moist, perfectly sautéed chicken breasts and something that turns out similar to the bottom of a well-worn shoe.

CHICKEN BREASTS and CANDIED ONIONS

2–4 servings

3 tablespoons fruit-scented vinegar (such as
    strawberry, blueberry, or raspberry)
¼ cup currants
1¼ cups heavy cream
3 tablespoons butter
1 pound tiniest pearl onions, peeled
1 cup chicken stock
2 whole chicken breasts (about 2 pounds),
    boned, skinned, and halved
Salt and black pepper to taste
Watercress for garnish

1. Combine the vinegar and currants and
marinate for at least 30 minutes.

2. In a saucepan over medium-high heat,
cook the cream until it is reduced by half.
Set aside to cool.

3. Melt 1 tablespoon of the butter in a large
sauté pan or heavy skillet over medium heat.
Add the onions and sauté until golden
brown. Lower the heat to medium and stir in
¼ cup of the stock. Cover and simmer for
about 5 minutes, or until the onions are
tender.

4. Stir in the vinegar and currants. Continue
cooking, uncovered, until the onions are
glazed and the moisture in the pan has
almost evaporated completely. Remove the
onions to a dish and keep warm.

5. In the same pan over medium-high heat
melt the remaining 2 tablespoons of butter.
Sauté the chicken breasts for 3 to 5 minutes
on each side. Do not overcook. Transfer the
chicken breasts to a heated platter and keep
warm.

6. Add to the pan the remaining ¾ cup stock
and cook over high heat until the liquid is reduced by half. Remove the pan from the fire
and stir in the cream. Heat the sauce
through. Season with salt and pepper.

7. Pour a small amount of sauce on the bottom of a heated serving platter. Put the
chicken breasts on the sauce. Arrange the
watercress at the eges of the platter. Spoon
the remaining sauce over the chicken breasts,
and place candied onions in between.

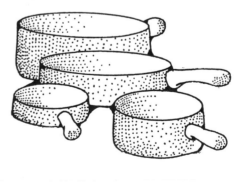

CHICKEN BREASTS with MUSHROOMS AND CREAM

This is a particularly elegant dish— great for company.

2–4 servings

6 tablespoons (¾ stick) butter
2 whole chicken breasts (about 2 pounds), skinned, boned, and halved
Salt and black pepper to taste
2 tablespoons finely minced shallots
1 small garlic clove, finely minced
3 cups thinly sliced mushrooms, washed and stems removed
2 tablespoons fresh lemon juice
White pepper to taste
¾ cup dry white wine
¾ cup chicken stock
1 cup heavy cream

1. In a sauté pan or heavy skillet over medium-high heat, melt 4 tablespoons of the butter. Add the chicken breasts, sprinkle with salt and pepper, and sauté for 3 to 5 minutes on each side, or until lightly browned. Remove to a dish and set aside.

2. Reduce the heat to medium and melt the remaining 2 tablespoons of butter in the same pan. Add the shallots and garlic; cook until tender but not browned. Add the mushrooms, lemon juice, and white pepper. Continue cooking until the mushroom liquid has almost completely evaporated.

3. Add the wine and chicken stock and continue cooking until the liquid has almost evaporated. Reduce the heat to medium-low, stir in the cream, and cook, uncovered, for about 5 minutes, or until the sauce begins to thicken.

4. Return the chicken breasts to the sauce to heat through. Place on a serving platter and spoon on the mushroom cream sauce.

CHICKEN BREASTS WITH MUSHROOMS AND COGNAC Eliminate the lemon juice. In step 3, substitute ½ cup warmed Cognac for the wine and increase the stock to 1 cup. Garnish with sprigs of fresh parsley.

THE MEANING OF SAUTE *EN FRANCAISE*

The French verb *sauter* means to jump or to leap. A grasshopper—the crooked-legged insect that seemingly is propelled with rocket force—is called *la sauterelle*.

In cooking, *sauter* or *sauté* means to cook over high heat with a small amount of fat, so that the food "jumps" with force in the pan as it cooks. If your chicken breasts aren't jumping slightly during the sauté methods of cooking, either there's too much fat in the pan or the fire isn't high enough.

SUPREMES DE VOLAILLE DEJA-VU

In the city of Philadelphia, on Pine Street, there is a deliciously romantic little restaurant named Déjà-Vu. The chef and owner, Solomon Montezinos, can be found creating some of the most tantalizing and terrific dishes imaginable. Suprêmes de Volaille Déjà-Vu is one. Solomon suggests serving this dish with a julienne of turnips, sautéed in a little butter, Champagne vinegar, and a bit of brown sugar.

2–4 servings

½ cup currants
¼ cup Marsala wine
2 tablespoons (¼ stick) clarified butter
2 whole chicken breasts (about 2 pounds), boned, skinned, and halved
1 tablespoon Madeira wine
1 tablespoon Cognac
2 tablespoons heavy cream
1 tablespoon orange blossom honey
1 teaspoon paprika
2 teaspoons water-packed green peppercorns, drained
2 tablespoons (¼ stick) butter
1 large shallot, chopped
1 garlic clove, minced
½ pound fresh egg noodles, cooked and drained
Salt and black pepper to taste

1. Put the currants, Marsala and ¼ cup of water in a small saucepan and poach until currants are soft. Remove the saucepan from the heat and set aside.

2. Melt the clarified butter in a sauté pan or heavy skillet over medium-high heat. Sauté the chicken breasts for 2 to 3 minutes on each side, or until lightly browned. Do not overcook. Transfer the chicken breasts to a heated platter and keep warm in the oven, set on low.

3. Remove any excess fat from the pan, set over medium heat, and add the Madeira and Cognac. Stir in the cream, honey, and paprika. Continue cooking until reduced by a quarter of the original amount. Strain the liquid from the currants and add it to the sauce. Stir in the currents and green peppercorns and set aside. Heat the dinner plates.

4. In another skillet over high heat, melt 2 tablespoons butter and quickly sauté the shallot and garlic. Add the cooked noodles and toss to heat through. Season with salt and pepper. Keep warm.

5. Remove the chicken breasts from the oven. If any juice has collected on the plate, stir it into the noodles. Cut the chicken breasts lengthwise into ⅓-inch-wide strips.

6. Put the hot noodles on dinner plates, place the chicken strips over the noodles, and spoon on the sauce.

CHICKEN BREASTS LA FOLIE

Luckily, advanced training at the Cordon Bleu School of Cooking is not necessary to perform the steps involved in making this recipe—only elementary cooking techniques, and a fondness for the taste of chicken breasts. This recipe, though fancy in flavor, will take you from lighting the stove to lighting the candles at the dinner table in half an hour or less. Chicken Breasts La Folie is one of the prize recipes of Bernard Norget, chef of *Grande Cuisine,* who suggests serving it with linguine, green beans, snow peas, and lots and lots and lots of ice-cold Champagne. Thank you, Bernard, for this tasty triumph.

2–4 servings

3 shallots, chopped
2 tablespoons chopped fresh tarragon leaves
6 turns of the pepper mill
1 cup dry white wine
¼ cup tarragon vinegar
3 drops Worcestershire sauce
2 whole chicken breasts (about 2 pounds), skinned and boned
Salt and black pepper to taste
2 tablespoons butter
1½ cups heavy cream

1. In a small saucepan over low heat, cook the shallots, tarragon, pepper, ⅔ cup of the white wine, vinegar, and Worcestershire sauce until the ingredients are reduced and the bottom of the saucepan is almost dry. Set the pan aside.

2. Season the chicken breasts with salt and pepper. In a sauté pan or heavy skillet over medium-high heat, melt the butter until hot and foamy. Sauté the chicken breasts for 2 to 3 minutes on each side, or just until lightly browned. Do not overcook.

3. Pour the remaining ⅓ cup of white wine into the sauté pan, add the reduced sauce mixture, and continue cooking until most of the moisture has evaporated from the sauté pan.

4. Lower the fire, add the cream, and continue cooking, turning occasionally, for about 7 minutes, or until the chicken breasts are tender. Remove to a heated platter. Taste for seasoning and spoon the sauce over the chicken breasts.

CHICKEN BREASTS with MORELS AND PECANS

Though expensive, morels are wonderful little wild mushrooms, and until you taste them, your palate cannot understand the absolutely amazing flavor they impart. Buy morels in specialty food stores.

2–4 servings

½ cup (½ ounce) dried morels, softened
    (see below)
4 tablespoons clarified butter (page 10)
2 whole chicken breasts (about 2 pounds),
    skinned, boned, and halved
Pinch of salt
Black pepper to taste
1 tablespoon minced prosciutto
3 tablespoons Cognac
2 tablespoons (¼ stick) butter
⅓ cup coarsely chopped pecan halves
1 cup chicken stock
½ cup heavy cream

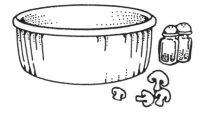

1. To soften the morels, put in hot water for 30 minutes; drain and dry.

2. In a sauté pan or heavy skillet over medium-high heat, melt the clarified butter. Sauté the chicken breasts for 2 to 3 minutes on each side, or until lightly browned. Do not overcook. Sprinkle with salt and pepper.

3. Reduce heat to medium-low; add the prosciutto, 2 tablespoons of the Cognac, and the morels. Mix well, cover, and cook until the chicken breasts are firm, about 5 minutes. Transfer the chicken breasts and morels to a heated platter and keep warm.

4. In a small heavy skillet over medium heat, melt the butter. Sauté the pecans until lightly browned and slightly crispy. Set aside.

5. Remove most of the fat from the pan. Over high heat, add the stock and cook until reduced by half. Lower the heat to medium, stir in the cream and the remaining 1 tablespoon of Cognac, and simmer until the sauce has thickened slightly. Spoon the sauce over the chicken breasts and morels. Sprinkle with the toasted pecans.

"An empty stomach will not listen to anything."

Spanish proverb

INDIAN SPICE CHICKEN

Fred Eversley has several reputations to live up to. First, as an artist—he sculpts magnificent objects from acrylic, steel, and sometimes neon. And second, as an incredibly inventive cook, Indian cuisine being one of his specialties. This recipe is a particular favorite of his. Fred insists on cooking Indian Spice Chicken Breasts in January as well as July, for 2 to 22 people. This is also a recipe that can be doubled or even tripled as the guest list grows.

6 servings

1 ½ cups plain yogurt
1 small onion, minced
1 teaspoon powdered cumin
1 teaspoon *garam masala* (see Note)
1 ¼ teaspoons salt
¾ teaspoon powdered turmeric
¼ teaspoon minced ginger
3 whole chicken breasts (about 3 pounds), halved
4 tablespoons clarified butter (see page 10)
2 large onions, thinly sliced
4 garlic cloves, minced
1 tablespoon tomato paste
1 ¼ teaspoons red pepper flakes
6 cups cooked white rice (see page 37)

1. In a large bowl, combine ½ cup of the yogurt, the onion, cumin, *garam masala,* salt, turmeric, and ginger. Mix together thoroughly. Add the chicken breasts, coating well. Marinate for at least 1 hour at room temperature; stir occasionally.

2. In a heavy skillet over medium-high heat, melt the clarified butter. Add the sliced onions and sauté until golden brown. Add the garlic and sauté for 1 minute more. Stir in the tomato paste. Add the chicken pieces and marinade; combine thoroughly. Cook, covered, for 5 minutes. Lower the heat and simmer for 10 minutes more.

3. Stir in the remaining yogurt, and sprinkle on the red pepper flakes. Simmer, covered, for another 10 minutes. Transfer the chicken breasts to a heated platter with cooked rice on it. Spoon the sauce and onions over the chicken breast pieces and rice.

Note *Garam masala* is a powdered mixture of cardamom seeds, cinnamon, cloves, pepper, and nutmeg. It is available at Indian food stores.

Stir-Frying

This Chinese cooking method is perfect for chicken breasts, since it takes but a few minutes to toss the chicken pieces over the very hot surfaces of the wok; they won't dry out, either, because they are cooked so quickly. In many recipes, the chicken breast pieces are stir-fried first, then removed from the wok while the other ingredients are tossed to doneness. The chicken is returned to the wok to be combined with the other ingredients just before the finish.

A successful stir-fry can be accomplished in 2 or 3 minutes so long as all the ingredients are chopped, sliced, diced, or slivered in advance. The Chinese use a cleaver for chopping the ingredients, but a large, very sharp chef's knife will do the job as well.

The best oils to use for stir-fry cooking are corn, safflower, peanut, and cottonseed, because they remain odorless when heated to a high temperature. Do not use olive oil or butter, which impart their own distinctive flavors to food.

Other ingredients called for in Chinese cooking are ground red pepper paste *(sambal oeleck),* sesame oil, ginger root, bok choy (Chinese cabbage), and soy sauce, all of which can be found in Oriental markets or special sections of many supermarkets.

Use ground red pepper paste with caution—it is fiery—and use sesame oil as a flavor enhancer or garnish, not as an oil for stir-frying. Always peel ginger root as the first step in its preparation.

Finally, it is wise to gather those who will be partaking in the feast prior to starting the stir-frying. Ready to eat in a flash, these dishes should be served immediately. Reheating makes them unpleasantly overcooked.

CHICKEN with CHINESE VEGETABLES

2–4 servings

1 whole chicken breast (about 1 pound),
    skinned, boned, and diced
1 egg white
½ teaspoon soy sauce
½ teaspoon salt
1 tablespoon cornstarch
½ cup vegetable oil
2 tablespoons (¼ stick) butter
¾ cup whole blanched almonds
½ cup mild rice wine vinegar
3 tablespoons sugar
⅛ teaspoon salt
1 cup finely chopped celery
1 cup chopped bok choy, blanched, drained,
    and dried
½ cup fresh peas, shelled, blanched,
    drained, and dried
½ cup julienned bell pepper
1 tablespoon cornstarch dissolved in 2
    tablespoons water

1. Combine the chicken, egg white, soy sauce, and salt; sprinkle with cornstarch. Marinate for 15 minutes.

2. Put the oil in a wok over a medium-high fire. When the oil is hot but not smoking, add the chicken breast mixture and stir-fry for 1 minute, or until lightly browned. Remove the chicken with a slotted spoon, drain, and set aside.

3. In a small skillet over medium heat, melt the butter. Sauté the almonds until brown. Set aside.

4. In a bowl, combine the vinegar, sugar, and salt. Remove all but 1 tablespoon of oil from the wok. Over medium-high heat, stir-fry the celery, bok choy, peas, and bell pepper. Add the vinegar mixture and continue stir-frying for a few seconds. Add the cornstarch paste and stir until the sauce thickens. Add the chicken and almonds, and toss to heat through.

HOW TO MAKE ORIENTAL CHICKEN STOCK

3 pounds raw chicken carcasses, necks, legs,
    gizzards, hearts, and trimmings
1 tablespoon rice wine or dry sherry
4 slices of ginger root, about 1 inch in diameter
    and ⅛ inch thick
4 large scallions, chopped
8 cups of water
Salt, to taste

1. Put the chicken pieces in a large saucepan. Add wine, ginger, scallions, salt and water and bring to a rapid boil over high heat. With a tablespoon, skim off the foam that floats to the top.

2. Simmer, covered, over low heat for 3 hours. Strain the stock, using a fine strainer or a piece of cheesecloth, and let cool. If you're not planning to use the stock right away, freeze it in plastic containers. Or freeze it in ice cube trays and transfer the cubes to plastic bags.

CANTONESE LEMON CHICKEN

2–4 servings

1 whole chicken breast (about 1 pound),
    skinned, boned, and cut into 1 x 2-inch
    pieces about ¼ inch thick
1 tablespoon dry sherry
1½ tablespoons soy sauce
1 tablespoon cornstarch
1 egg white
1 cup vegetable oil
1 teaspoon minced ginger root
½ cup chicken stock
2 tablespoons lemon juice
½ tablespoon sugar
¼ teaspoon salt
1 teaspoon cornstarch dissolved in 2
    tablespoons water
½ tablespoon lemon rind
1 thinly sliced lemon

1. In a bowl, combine the chicken, sherry, 1 tablespoon soy sauce, cornstarch, and egg white. Marinate for 15 minutes.

2. Heat the oil in a wok over medium-high heat. When the oil is very hot but not smoking, drop in the chicken and marinade; stir-fry for 2 minutes, or until the chicken begins to turn white. Remove with a slotted spoon, drain, and set aside.

3. Remove all but 1 tablespoon of oil from the wok. Add the ginger and stir-fry for about 30 seconds.

4. Add the stock, lemon juice, sugar, salt, and remaining ½ tablespoon of soy sauce and bring to a boil. Stir in the cornstarch paste and continue stirring until the sauce thickens. Add the lemon rind and return the chicken breast pieces to the sauce. Stir-fry to heat through. Turn onto a heated platter and garnish with lemon slices.

HOW TO MAKE PERFECT WHITE RICE

Rice cookery and its many methods could fill a volume. This is one typical Chinese rice-cooking technique:

For 3 cups of cooked rice, put 1 cup of long-grain white rice in a saucepan. Rinse the rice by covering it with water. Pour off the rinse water and add 1¾ cups of water to the rice, along with ½ teaspoon of salt. Bring the water to a boil, cook for 2 minutes, then cover the saucepan, reduce the heat to very low, and cook for 20 minutes. Remove the rice from the heat and allow to "set" for 10 minutes. Stir to separate the rice grains before serving.

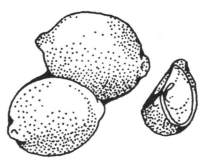

KUNG PAO CHICKEN

2–4 servings

Sauce

4 tablespoons soy sauce
1 ½ tablespoons cornstarch
2 tablespoons sugar
2 tablespoons sesame oil
4 tablespoons chicken stock
1 teaspoon Chinese red pepper sauce (*sambal oeleck*)

2 whole chicken breasts (about 2 pounds), skinned, boned, and cut into 1-inch cubes
1 egg white
1 tablespoon sherry
1 tablespoon cornstarch
3 tablespoons vegetable oil
16 scallions (white part only), cut into ½-inch lengths
16 very thin slices ginger root, quartered
1 cup roasted unsalted peanuts

1. Combine the sauce ingredients and set aside.

2. In a bowl, combine the chicken, egg white, sherry, and cornstarch. Marinate for 15 minutes.

3. Over medium-high heat, heat the oil in a wok until very hot but not smoking. Add the chicken and marinade; stir-fry for 3 minutes. Remove the chicken with a slotted spoon, drain, and set aside.

4. Add the scallions and ginger to the wok and stir-fry for 30 seconds. Add the sauce and heat through. Return the chicken to the wok, along with the peanuts. Continue stir-frying for about 1 minute, or until the sauce thickens.

ADVANCE PREPARATION—THE SECRET OF SUCCESSFUL STIR-FRYING

Several of the Chinese recipes in this chapter were contributed by Bert Gader (whose Chinese cooking classes I attended in Los Angeles). Bert, boasting some twenty-five hundred Chinese recipes in his card file, has gone so far as to make a science of cooking and serving this cuisine. And because of his extraordinary emphasis on advance planning and preparation (which is the secret to the successful stir-fry), he has developed a method of turning out an impressive five- or six-course Cantonese or Szechwan meal for ten from stove to table in ten minutes. Sporting a white linen suit with antique watch fob hanging from his waistcoat pocket, this 100 percent Jewish "artist of the wok and steamer" seats his guests at the long dining table of dark wood. By the time each Lalique crystal wineglass is filled, he is bursting forth from the kitchen with dish after platter after bowl of Kung Pao Chicken, Spicy Eggplant, Steamed Custard, and more. Many of his standard recipes revolve around chicken breasts—indispensable in Chinese cuisine—and Bert has even said that the only cooking ingredients he buys more of than rice are chicken breasts.

WALNUT CHICKEN

2–4 servings

2 whole chicken breasts (about 2 pounds),
    skinned, boned, and cut into ½-inch
    cubes
2 tablespoons cornstarch
2 tablespoons dry sherry
1 egg white
2 tablespoons soy sauce
1 teaspoon sugar
½ teaspoon salt
4 teaspoons sesame oil
½ cup walnuts cut into quarters
1 teaspoon minced ginger root
1 tablespoon chopped scallions (white part
    only)

1. In a bowl, combine the chicken, corn-starch, sherry, and egg white. Marinate for 15 minutes. In another bowl, combine the soy sauce, sugar, and salt.

2. In a wok over medium-high heat, heat the oil until very hot but not smoking. Add the walnuts and stir-fry for 1 minute. Remove the walnuts with a slotted spoon and set aside.

3. Add the chicken and marinade to the wok and stir-fry for about 2 to 3 minutes. Add the ginger and scallions and continue stir-frying for about 30 seconds more.

4. Pour in the soy sauce, sugar, and salt mixture, stirring and tossing to combine. Stir in the walnuts and heat through.

STIR-FRIED RICE

2–4 servings

4 tablespoons vegetable oil
1 cup minced onions
1 whole chicken breast (about 1 pound),
    skinned, boned, and cut into 1-inch
    cubes
1 cup cooked long-grain rice, at room
    temperature
½ cup fresh peas, blanched
½ teaspoon salt
3 eggs, lightly beaten
6 scallions (white and some green part),
    chopped
3 to 4 tablespoons soy sauce, to taste

1. Heat the oil in a wok over medium-high heat until hot but not smoking. Add the onions and stir-fry for 2 to 3 minutes, or until soft and lightly browned. Add the chicken, stir-frying for another 2 minutes, or until the chicken turns white.

2. Add the rice, peas, and salt, stirring and tossing to heat through. Push the mixture to the sides of the wok; pour the eggs into the center. Cook the eggs, stirring for about 30 seconds. Toss the rice and eggs together. Add the scallions, sprinkle on the soy sauce, mix, and heat through. Serve immediately.

CHICKEN with BROCCOLI

From Joan Wenzel.

2-4 servings

1 whole chicken breast (about 1 pound),
    skinned, boned, and cut into 1 x 2-inch
    pieces
½ tablespoon rice wine or sherry
½ teaspoon salt
1 tablespoon soy sauce
Dash of white pepper
½ tablespoon cornstarch
½ cup vegetable oil
3 cups broccoli, cut into small pieces
½ cup chicken stock
1 teaspoon cornstarch dissolved in 1
    tablespoon water

1. In a small bowl, combine the chicken, wine, half the salt, soy sauce, white pepper, and cornstarch. Marinate for 15 minutes or longer.

2. Heat the oil in a wok over medium-high heat. When the oil is very hot but not smoking, add the chicken and marinade; stir-fry for 1 minute, or until the chicken begins to turn white. Remove with a slotted spoon, drain, and set aside.

3. Remove all but 1 tablespoon of oil from the wok. Add the broccoli and the remaining salt and stir-fry for 30 seconds. Add the stock, cover, and cook for 2 minutes.

4. Uncover, stir in the cornstarch paste, and stir-fry until the sauce begins to thicken. Return the chicken breast pieces to the wok and stir-fry for 30 seconds to heat through.

PLUM CHICKEN

2-4 servings

1 tablespoon sugar
3 tablespoons cornstarch
2 tablespoons dry sherry
¼ teaspoon ground ginger
⅛ teaspoon black pepper
¾ cup chicken stock
2 tablespoons soy sauce
1 tablespoon lemon juice

1 tablespoon white wine vinegar
3 tablespoons vegetable oil
1 whole chicken breast (about 1 pound),
    skinned, boned, and julienned
1 cup thinly sliced Bermuda (red) onion
1 cup thinly sliced celery (cut on the
    diagonal)
¼ teaspoon minced garlic
6 large ripe plums, halved and seeded

1. In a saucepan, combine the sugar, cornstarch, sherry, ginger, black pepper, stock, soy sauce, lemon juice, and vinegar. Over medium-low heat, cook the sauce ingredients for 2 minutes, or until the sauce begins to thicken. Set aside.

2. Heat the oil in a wok over medium-high heat until hot but not smoking. Add the chicken and stir-fry for 2 minutes, or until it begins to turn white. Remove with a slotted spoon, drain, and set aside.

3. Add to the wok the onion, celery, and garlic; stir-fry until the vegetables are lightly glazed, about 1 minute.

4. Add the plums, toss the ingredients together gently, and cook over a low fire for about 3 minutes, or until the plums are soft. Return the chicken and the sauce to the wok. Heat through with the other ingredients.

MOO GOO GAI PAN

Bert Gader suggests serving this dish with white rice (see page 37), sprinkled generously with sliced almonds sautéed in a little butter.

2 servings

1 whole chicken breast (about 1 pound), skinned, boned, and cut into 1-inch cubes
2 tablespoons cornstarch
1 egg white
1 tablespoon dry sherry
¼ teaspoon salt
¼ teaspoon black pepper
⅓ cup chicken stock
2 tablespoons vegetable oil
3 thin slices ginger root, minced
1 garlic clove, minced
½ pound mushrooms, washed and stems removed
5 water chestnuts, thinly sliced

1. In a bowl, combine the chicken, 1 tablespoon of the cornstarch, the egg white, sherry, salt, and pepper. Marinate for 15 minutes. Combine the stock and the remaining 1 tablespoon of cornstarch. Set aside.

2. Heat the oil in a wok over medium-high heat until very hot but not smoking. Add the ginger and garlic and stir-fry for 1 minute. Add the chicken and marinade and continue stir-frying for 3 minutes, or just until the chicken begins to turn brown. Add the mushrooms and stir-fry for 1 minute more.

3. Stir the stock and cornstarch mixture into the wok; cook for about 30 seconds, or until the sauce thickens. Add in the water chestnuts and heat through.

SZECHWAN ORANGE CHICKEN

A hot and spicy combination of flavors! To cool down the "Szechwan" in this recipe, reduce the amounts of red chili peppers and roasted peppercorns considerably—or turn to the next recipe!

2–4 servings

2 whole chicken breasts (about 2 pounds), skinned, boned, and cut into 1-inch cubes
1 teaspoon cornstarch
¾ cup chopped onion
4 scallions, cut lengthwise into 1-inch pieces
3 small red chili peppers, minced
2 teaspoons finely crushed oven-roasted Szechwan peppercorns
2 teaspoons minced ginger root
2 tablespoons orange juice
2 tablespoons soy sauce
1 tablespoon hoisin sauce
½ teaspoon sugar
½ teaspoon Szechwan chili paste with garlic
7 tablespoons vegetable oil
2 tablespoons fresh orange peel cut into *very* fine threads
1 teaspoon white wine vinegar
1 teaspoon sesame oil

1. In a bowl combine the chicken and cornstarch. In another bowl combine the onion and the scallions. In another bowl, combine the chili peppers, peppercorns, and ginger. In yet another bowl, stir together the orange juice, soy sauce, hoisin sauce, sugar, and chili paste; mix well. Set all four bowls aside.

2. Heat the oil in a wok over medium-high heat until hot but not smoking. Add the chicken and stir-fry about 2 minutes, or just until it turns white; remove with a slotted spoon, drain, and set aside.

3. Remove all but 1 tablespoon of oil from the wok. Turn the heat up to high. Add the chili pepper mixture, stir-frying for 15 seconds. Add the orange peel and onions and stir-fry for another 30 seconds.

4. Working quickly, add the cooked chicken and the juice mixture; stir-fry for another 30 seconds. Then add the vinegar, stirring and tossing to combine the ingredients; cook for an additional 15 seconds. At the very end, mix in the sesame oil and turn onto a heated platter.

CHICKEN with SHIITAKE MUSHROOMS

The flavor of this Szechwan-style dish is hot and sour. Shiitake mushrooms, add an interesting subtle flavor and texture to the dish. Typically, shiitake mushrooms are sold dried and must be rehydrated before being cooked.

2–4 servings

2 whole chicken breasts (about 2 pounds), skinned, boned, and cut into 1½-inch pieces
1½ teaspoons finely crushed oven-roasted Szechwan peppercorns
6 tablespoons rice wine vinegar
1 tablespoon soy sauce
½ teaspoon sugar
4 tablespoons vegetable oil
6 large shiitake mushrooms (about 1 ounce dried), softened in hot water for 30 minutes, rinsed, drained, and squeezed dry
2 scallions (white and some green part), chopped
1 large garlic clove, minced
1 teaspoon minced ginger
1 cup chicken stock
1 teaspoon sesame oil
Coriander leaves for garnish (optional)

1. In a bowl, combine the chicken, ½ teaspoon of the crushed peppercorns, 2 tablespoons of the vinegar, and the soy sauce and sugar. Marinate for 30 minutes. Drain the chicken and reserve the marinade.

2. Heat the oil in a wok over medium-high heat until hot but not smoking. Add the chicken and stir-fry about 3 minutes, or until browned. Remove with a slotted spoon, drain, and set aside.

3. Trim the tough stems off the mushrooms. (Check to see that no sand particles remain, if so, use a vegetable brush to remove). Slice the mushrooms ¼ inch thick.

4. Remove all but 1 tablespoon of oil from the wok and return the heat to medium-high. Add the scallions, garlic, and ginger and stir-fry about 30 seconds, or until the scallions begin to brown slightly. Return the chicken to the wok, add the mushrooms, and reduce the heat to low. Cook for about 5 minutes, or until the chicken pieces are firm. Remove to a heated serving platter and keep warm.

5. Over medium-high heat, add to the wok the chicken stock and the remaining 1 teaspoon of Szechwan peppercorns and 4 tablespoons of vinegar. Bring to a boil and cook for about 2 minutes, or until reduced by half. Pour over the chicken and sprinkle with sesame oil. Garnish the platter with fresh coriander leaves.

CHINESE CHICKEN BREASTS WRAPPED IN LETTUCE LEAVES

Perfect for finger food or hors d'oeuvres, even a main dish. The final flavors are hot and spicy in the Szechwan style.

2–4 servings

1 whole chicken breast (about 1 pound), skinned, boned, and cut into 1½ x ⅛-inch pieces
1 egg white
2 teaspoons cornstarch
2 tablespoons medium sherry or Chinese rice wine
1 teaspoon salt
16 curly-edged lettuce leaves, washed, dried with paper towels, and refrigerated
4 tablespoons vegetable oil
2 teaspoons finely chopped ginger root
1 teaspoon Chinese chili sauce (or ¼ teaspoon hot red pepper flakes)
1 teaspoon cornstarch dissolved in 2 tablespoons chicken stock
¼ cup pine nuts, toasted in a 350° F. oven for 10 minutes

1. In a bowl, combine the chicken, egg white, 2 teaspoons cornstarch, sherry, and salt. Toss together thoroughly to coat the chicken. Cover and marinate for 30 minutes.

2. Arrange the lettuce leaves on a serving platter; cover lightly and refrigerate until ready to use.

3. Heat the oil in a wok over medium-high heat until hot but not smoking. Add the ginger and stir-fry for 1 minute. Add the chicken and marinade, stir-frying for 1 minute more, or until the chicken begins to turn white. Add the chili sauce and stir-fry for about 30 seconds more.

4. Stir in the cornstarch paste and cook until it thickens. Turn the ingredients onto a heated serving platter, sprinkle with pine nuts, and eat, finger-food style, wrapped in lettuce leaves.

HOISIN CHICKEN

From Gregory Lynn, who recommends serving this dish hot as a main course or cold as a very interesting appetizer. Slices of papaya splashed with lemon juice are the perfect accompaniment.

4–6 servings

2 whole chicken breasts (about 2 pounds), skinned, boned, pounded to ¼ inch thick, and cut into ½-inch-wide strips

Marinade
Juice of 1 lemon
Juice of 1 small lime
2 tablespoons hoisin sauce
2 tablespoons black bean sauce (canned)
⅛ teaspoon ground ginger
Juice of 1 garlic clove
Dash of nutmeg
Dash of cinnamon
2 tablespoons soy sauce

4 ounces sesame seeds
6 tablespoons vegetable oil
½ pound fresh asparagus, tough bottom part trimmed off, sliced very thin on the diagonal
6 whole water chestnuts (canned), thinly sliced
½ pound snow peas, strings removed, blanched and drained
4 tablespoons cornstarch

1. Combine the chicken with the marinade ingredients. Cover and refrigerate for at least 2 hours.

2. In a large skillet over medium-high heat, cook the sesame seeds, stirring constantly, for about 6 to 8 minutes, or until they are browned and start to pop. Quickly remove the seeds from the skillet, to stop the cooking, and set aside.

3. Drain the chicken and reserve the marinade. Heat the oil in a wok over medium-high heat until hot but not smoking. Add the chicken and 1 ounce of the sesame seeds and stir-fry for about 2 minutes, or just until the chicken begins to turn white. Remove and set aside.

4. Add to the wok the asparagus and water chestnuts and cook for 1 minute. Add the snow peas and cook for 1 more minute, stirring occasionally.

5. Combine the reserved marinade with the cornstarch and add to the wok, stirring until the sauce thickens. Return the chicken to the wok and heat through, tossing and stirring until the sauce has completely thickened. Spoon the chicken mixture over papaya slices sprinkled with the remaining sesame seeds.

Grilling and Broiling

C hicken breasts are among the best foods suited to summer backyard parties and picnics—especially when marinated and then cooked over white-hot coals or under the direct flames of a broiler. Luckily, its tenderness and taste never reflect the paucity of time you put into the preparation. Cooperative by nature, chicken breasts absorb the flavors of marinades instantly. They also need far less time over the coals to reach a perfect state of doneness than perhaps any other meat. So, with a few ounces of interesting ingredients and a few pounds of chicken breasts—and, of course, a barbecue filled with white-hot coals—you can take the grand gourmet taste outdoors.

SPICY PEANUT CHICKEN

2–4 servings

½ cup smooth peanut butter (100 percent peanuts—no salt or sugar added)
5 tablespoons soy sauce
1 tablespoon brown sugar
2 tablespoons water
2 garlic cloves, minced
1 tablespoon fresh lemon juice
1 teaspoon dried crushed red chilies (or ½ teaspoon chili flakes)
½ teaspoon ground cinnamon
4 tablespoons (½ stick) butter
1 onion, chopped
2 whole chicken breasts (about 2 pounds), halved

1. In a blender or food processor, combine the peanut butter, soy sauce, brown sugar, water, garlic, lemon juice, chilies, and cinnamon.

2. Put the mixture in a saucepan over low heat. Add the butter and melt; simmer for 5 minutes. Let cool to room temperature.

3. Put the onion and chicken breasts in a single layer in a shallow glass or ceramic dish. Pour on the marinade and let stand, covered, for 12 to 24 hours in the refrigerator.

4. Prepare the grill or heat the broiler. Cook the chicken about 7 to 8 inches from the flame for about 4 to 5 minutes on each side, turning several times during the cooking process.

SESAME–LEMON CHICKEN

4 servings

½ cup light soy sauce (Japanese style)
½ cup lemon juice
2 teaspoons sesame oil
1 teaspoon sugar
¼ teaspoon salt
2 whole chicken breasts (about 2 pounds), halved

1. In a bowl, combine the soy sauce, lemon juice, sesame oil, sugar, and salt.

2. Arrange the chicken breasts in a single layer in a shallow glass or ceramic dish. Pour on the marinade and let stand at room temperature for 1 hour, turning and basting frequently.

3. Prepare the grill or heat the broiler. Cook the chicken breasts 6 to 8 inches from the heat for 4 to 6 minutes on each side, starting with the bone side toward the heat. Baste and turn several times during the cooking process.

CHINESE MARINADE

Enough for 2 pounds of chicken breasts

3 tablespoons soy sauce
2 tablespoons honey
2 tablespoons hoisin sauce
2 tablespoons white wine vinegar
2 tablespoons rice wine or pale dry sherry
1 teaspoon crushed garlic
1 teaspoon minced ginger root

1 teaspoon sugar
2 tablespoons chicken stock
2 tablespoons Chinese plum sauce (available in Oriental markets)

Marinate chicken breasts in the above ingredients for at least 2 hours before grilling or broiling.

LONE STAR BBQ SAUCE

From Mark Erwin, who was raised on this special Texas-style sauce. Serve hot or cold.

4–6 servings

3 whole chicken breasts (about 3 pounds), halved
¼ cup vinegar
1 teaspoon salt
½ teaspoon crushed garlic
1 tablespoon brown sugar
¼ teaspoon black pepper
8 tablespoons (1 stick) butter
1 medium onion, chopped
1 tablespoon prepared mustard (Dijon-style is very nice)
Juice of ½ lemon
1 teaspoon chili powder
¼ cup chili sauce
3 tablespoons Worcestershire sauce
¼ bottle beer

1. Put the chicken breasts, skin side up, in a single layer in a shallow glass or ceramic dish.

2. In a small saucepan over low heat, combine the vinegar, salt, garlic, brown sugar, black pepper, butter, onion, mustard, lemon juice, and chili powder. Simmer for 5 minutes and remove from the heat.

3. Add to the saucepan the chili sauce, Worcestershire sauce, and beer. Bring to a boil and remove from the heat.

4. Brush the chicken breasts with the barbecue sauce and let stand at room temperature for 30 minutes.

5. Prepare the barbecue or oven broiler. Place the chicken breasts, starting bone side toward the heat source, on the grill, 7 to 9 inches from the coals. Baste frequently and turn several times during the cooking process. Cook for 8 to 10 minutes, or until the barbecue sauce turns very brown and crispy.

SWEET AND SAVORY BUTTER-BASTED CHICKEN BREASTS

Happily, quick never means dull or boring or flavorless with this delectable white meat, especially when it's teamed up with a dollop of flavored butter.

The steps involved are few and uncomplicated. Simply pluck the herb butter from the freezer, melt it, and brush it on the chicken breast. Grill or broil for about 5 minutes on each side, starting with the bone side toward the fire. That's it!

Make several butters in advance so that when time is of the essence, they will be ready to help you make a memorable meal.

2 whole chicken breasts (about 2 pounds), skinned (optional) and halved
2 tablespoons flavored butter (recipes follow)

1. Preheat the oven broiler to very hot for about 15 minutes.

2. Remove the flavored butter from the freezer. Melt it in a saucepan over low heat.

3. Using a basting brush, coat the chicken breasts. Place under the broiler, starting with the bone side up, for 4 to 5 minutes, basting once more during cooking.

4. Turn the chicken breasts. Generously baste the skin (or skinned) side with the melted butter and continue broiling for 4 to 5 minutes more, or until done; baste once more during cooking. Serve hot or cold.

Garlic Butter

8 tablespoons (1 stick) butter
3 large garlic cloves, peeled
1 tablespoon olive oil
2 tablespoons grated Parmesan cheese (optional)
2 teaspoons fresh chives
1 teaspoon fresh basil leaves (or ¼ teaspoon dried)
Dash of salt and black pepper

Green Herb Butter

3 tablespoons finely chopped parsley (blanched, dried with paper towels, and then chopped)
2 tablespoons finely chopped spinach (blanched, dried with paper towels, and then chopped)
1 tablespoon each chopped fresh chervil, chives, and tarragon, blanched and dried with paper towels, and then chopped)
3 tablespoons chopped shallots
8 tablespoons (1 stick) butter
Salt and black pepper

Chutney Butter

8 tablespoons (1 stick) butter
3 tablespoons vegetable or fruit chutney (such as tomato, mango, peach)
1 teaspoon fresh lemon juice
Dash of cayenne pepper

Shallot Butter

4 shallots, blanched, dried with paper towels, and finely chopped
8 tablespoons (1 stick) butter
Salt and black pepper

Tarragon Butter

4 tablespoons fresh tarragon leaves, blanched and dried with paper towels
1 small garlic clove, finely minced
8 tablespoons (1 stick) butter
Salt and black pepper

Lime or Lemon Butter

1 shallot, blanched and dried with paper towels
2 teaspoons grated lime or lemon zest
1 tablespoon finely chopped fresh parsley
Dash of salt
White pepper to taste

Orange Spice Butter

8 tablespoons (1 stick) butter
2 tablespoons orange marmalade
1 tablespoon ground cinnamon
Dash of allspice

1. Put the ingredients for whichever flavored butter you are making in a food processor, blender, or blend together with a mortar and pestle. Mix well.

2. Freeze in small quantities (2 to 4 tablespoons), tightly wrapped in plastic sandwich bags or plastic wrap. Don't forget to mark the flavors on the packages.

Sweet Curry Butter

8 tablespoons (1 stick) butter
2 tablespoons honey
1 tablespoon curry powder

Mustard Butter

8 tablespoons (1 stick) butter
3 tablespoons Dijon-style (or other French) mustard
½ teaspoon fresh lemon juice
Dash of salt

INDONESIAN CHICKEN BREASTS

2–4 servings

¼ cup fresh lemon juice
2 tablespoons soy sauce
2 tablespoons brown sugar
2 garlic cloves, finely chopped
1 tablespoon peanut oil
2 whole chicken breasts (about 2 pounds),
    skinned, boned, halved, and cut into
    thirds lengthwise

Peanut Dipping Sauce

½ cup peanut butter (the type made of
    peanuts only)
1 garlic clove, minced
1 tablespoon brown sugar
1 cup fresh coconut milk
1 tablespoon lemon juice
¼ teaspoon salt

1. In a bowl, combine the lemon juice, soy sauce, brown sugar, garlic, and peanut oil; mix well. Add the chicken breast strips and marinate for at least 1 hour. Combine the dipping sauce ingredients in a saucepan and set aside.

2. Thread the chicken strips onto wooden skewers. Preheat the grill, hibachi, or broiler.

3. Over medium-high heat, bring the dipping sauce to a boil; reduce the heat and simmer for 2 minutes. Pour into a bowl.

4. Cook the chicken strips for about 2 minutes on each side, or until done. Serve immediately with hot dipping sauce.

MESQUITE OR PINE BOUGH SMOKED CHICKEN BREASTS

Mesquite or pine boughs add a rich and woody flavor to the chicken breasts. Served hot or cold, they are excellent.

2–4 servings

1 cup dry white wine
½ cup dry Spanish sherry

5 garlic cloves, coarsely chopped
1 medium onion, chopped
1 tablespoon brown sugar
Salt and black pepper to taste
2 whole chicken breasts (about 2 pounds),
    halved

4 to 5 pine boughs or ½ pound mesquite
    chips

1. In a food processor or blender, process the wine, sherry, garlic, onion, sugar, and salt and pepper until liquefied.

2. Arrange the chicken in a single layer in a shallow glass or ceramic dish. Pour on the marinade, cover, and refrigerate for 4 to 6 hours, turning several times.

3. Prepare the grill. When the coals are white-hot, add some of the pine boughs or mesquite chips to the fire and let the coals burn for 20 minutes more.

4. Arrange the chicken breasts on the grill, 7 to 9 inches from the coals. Cook for 4 to 5 minutes on each side, turning and basting several times with the marinade. Cook the chicken until it is crispy and brown.

HERB AND FRENCH MUSTARD BASTING SAUCE

4–6 servings

3 whole chicken breasts (about 3 pounds), skinned and halved
Salt and black pepper to taste

Mustard Herb Basting Sauce
3 tablespoons coarse French mustard (such as Moutarde de Meaux or Pommery)
2 egg yolks
1 scallion (white and some green part), chopped
1 teaspoon chopped fresh marjoram (or ¼ teaspoon dried)
2 tablespoons lemon juice
1 cup olive oil
½ cup heavy cream
1½ tablespoons capers, rinsed and drained

8 branches of fresh marjoram (for scattering on the coals)

1. Sprinkle the chicken breasts with salt and pepper.

2. In a food processor or blender, combine the mustard, egg yolks, scallion, marjoram, and lemon juice. Gradually add the oil and mix well. Add the cream and capers and blend well.

3. Put the chicken breasts in a single layer in a shallow glass or ceramic dish. Pour on the sauce and marinate for 30 minutes.

4. Prepare the barbecue grill, strewing the marjoram branches over the coals. Heat the coals to white-hot. Cook the chicken breast pieces on the grill 7 to 9 inches from the coals for 4 to 5 minutes on each side, turning and basting several times.

TANDOORI CHICKEN

4–6 servings

3 whole chicken breasts (about 3 pounds),
    halved
⅓ cup plus 2 tablespoons fresh lemon juice
1 teaspoon salt
½ teaspoon powdered saffron (or 2 saffron
    threads, minced)
2 teaspoons crushed coriander seeds
¼ teaspoon dried red pepper flakes
1 teaspoon cumin
2 large garlic cloves, coarsely chopped
1 teaspoon finely chopped ginger
1 cup plain yogurt
4 tablespoons (½ stick) butter

1. Prick the chicken breasts all over with a fork several times so the marinade can penetrate the breast meat.

2. Arrange the chicken breasts in a single layer in a shallow glass or ceramic dish.

3. In a bowl, combine ⅓ cup of the lemon juice, salt, and saffron. With your hands, rub this mixture into the chicken breasts.

4. In a small skillet over medium heat, toast the coriander seeds, red pepper flakes, and cumin for about 2 minutes, stirring constantly. Place in a food processor; add the garlic, ginger, and 4 tablespoons of the yogurt, and blend for 30 seconds. Add the remaining yogurt, mix well, and pour over the chicken breasts. Cover tightly and marinate at room temperature for at least 12 hours (or 24 hours in the refrigerator), turning the breasts several times.

5. Prepare the grill or heat the broiler. In a small saucepan over medium heat, melt the butter. Remove the chicken from the marinade and drain off the excess. Baste the chicken breasts with the butter and grill 7 to 9 inches from the hot coals for 4 to 5 minutes on each side, starting with the bone side toward the heat.

6. When the chicken breasts are done, sprinkle with the remaining 2 tablespoons of lemon juice.

SPICY SESAME CHICKEN BREAST

4–6 servings

3 whole chicken breasts (about 3 pounds),
    boned and halved
Salt and black pepper to taste

Marinade
4 tablespoons (½ stick) butter, melted
¼ cup soy sauce
¼ cup dry white wine
1 teaspoon dried tarragon
1 teaspoon dry mustard
8 ounces sesame seeds

1. Sprinkle the chicken breast with salt and pepper.

2. In a bowl, mix together the melted butter, soy sauce, wine, tarragon, and mustard. Arrange the chicken breasts in a single layer in a shallow glass or ceramic dish. Pour on the marinade, and let stand at room temperature for at least 2 hours.

3. Prepare the grill or heat the broiler. Starting with the bone side toward the heat, cook 7 to 9 inches from the coals for 4 to 5 minutes on each side. Baste the chicken breasts and turn several times during the cooking process.

4. Just before the chicken is done, remove from the fire and roll in the sesame seeds until well coated; return the chicken breasts to the fire for 2 to 3 more minutes, or until the seeds have browned but are not burned.

RED WINE MARINADE

2–4 servings

2 whole chicken breasts (about 2 pounds), halved
Salt and black pepper to taste

Marinade
¼ cup olive oil
2 medium onions, chopped
1 cup tomato purée
1 teaspoon dried basil (or 1 tablespoon finely chopped fresh basil)
⅓ cup honey
¼ cup chicken stock
3 tablespoons Worcestershire sauce
1 teaspoon dry mustard
1 cup Italian dry red wine

1. Sprinkle the chicken breasts with salt and pepper.

2. In a heavy skillet over medium heat, heat the olive oil. Sauté the onions until soft. Add the tomato purée, basil, honey, stock, Worcestershire sauce, and mustard; mix together well. Reduce the heat to low and simmer for 15 minutes. Add the wine in the last minute of cooking and heat through. Let cool to room temperature.

3. Arrange the chicken breast pieces in a single layer in a shallow glass or ceramic dish; pour on the marinade and let stand at room temperature for 3 hours, turning several times to coat well.

4. Prepare the grill or heat the broiler. Beginning bone side down, cook the chicken breasts 7 to 9 inches from the coals for 4 to 5 minutes on each side, basting several times.

CHICKEN TERIYAKI

Though we associate the word *teri-yaki* with a particular sweet herb flavoring that is frequently used as a marinade, to the Japanese it is the technique of grilling food while basting with soy sauce and sweetened rice wine. In this recipe the chicken breasts are cooked slower and farther away from the coals to keep the soy sauce from caramelizing. Adjust your broiler, too.

2–4 servings

2 whole chicken breasts (about 2 pounds), halved
½ cup peanut oil
½ cup light soy sauce (Japanese style)
2 tablespoons fresh ginger root, peeled and grated
2 garlic cloves, finely chopped
1 tablespoon orange zest
¼ cup sweet cooking rice wine or medium sherry

1. Arrange the chicken breasts in a single layer in a shallow glass or ceramic dish.

2. In a bowl combine the oil, soy sauce, ginger, garlic, orange zest, and rice wine. Pour over the chicken, cover, and marinate for 12 hours at room temperature or 24 hours in the refrigerator.

3. When you are ready to cook the chicken breasts, prepare the grill or heat the broiler. Cook the chicken breasts at least 8 to 10 inches away from the fire for 7 to 8 minutes on each side, beginning bone side away from the heat. Turn and baste at least twice during the cooking process.

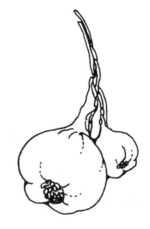

SWEET AND SOUR CHICKEN

4–6 servings

3 tablespoons vegetable oil
1 cup sugar
6 tablespoons soy sauce
2 cups red wine vinegar
2 tablespoons cornstarch
1 large onion, minced
3 tablespoons finely chopped ginger
3 whole chicken breasts (about 3 pounds),
    halved

1. In a saucepan, combine the oil, sugar, soy sauce, vinegar, and cornstarch. Over medium-high heat, bring to a boil and cook for 2 minutes.

2. Add the onion and ginger; continue to boil for 4 minutes more. Remove the sauce from the fire and let cool slightly.

3. Put the chicken breasts in a single layer in a shallow glass or ceramic dish and pour on the sauce. Marinate for 30 minutes to 1 hour.

4. Prepare the grill or heat the broiler. Cook the chicken breasts 7 to 9 inches from the flame for 4 to 5 minutes on each side, basting several times. Serve hot or cold.

SWEET AND SOUR PLUM MARINADE In step 1, add 1 cup pitted fresh plums. Strain the mixture before pouring over the chicken.

CHICKEN BREASTS with HERBS

2–4 servings

2 whole chicken breasts (about 2 pounds)
Herbs: 2 tablespoons of either fresh tarragon
    leaves or basil, or crushed dried rose-
    mary, or a combination of all of these
2 garlic cloves, peeled and quartered
1 large lemon, thinly sliced into rounds
4 tablespoons (½ stick) melted butter
Salt and black pepper to taste

1. Place the chicken breasts on a flat surface. Press down firmly with your palm to break the breastbone.

2. Carefully, without detaching the skin, place equal amounts of the herbs under the skin of each chicken breast. Push the pieces of garlic under the skin. Place lemon slices over the herbs and the garlic. Put the chicken breasts in a shallow pan and cover tightly; refrigerate for 12 hours or overnight.

3. Prepare the grill or heat the broiler. Remove the garlic and lemon slices from under the chicken skin, then rub the skin with butter and sprinkle with salt and pepper.

4. Cook the chicken 7 to 9 inches away from the fire for 6 to 8 minutes on each side, basting with melted butter several times during the cooking process.

WORCESTERSHIRE BASTING SAUCE

Enough for 4 to 5 pounds of chicken breasts

1 cup Worcestershire sauce
1 teaspoon pickling spice
½ teaspoon sugar
1 celery stalk (including top), chopped
1 onion, sliced
1 garlic clove, minced
1 cup water
½ cup vegetable oil
¼ cup dry sherry

1. In a stainless steel or enamel-coated sauce-pan combine the Worcestershire sauce, pickling spice, sugar, celery, onion, garlic, and water. Simmer for 25 minutes. In the last 5 minutes of cooking, add the oil and sherry. Let cool to room temperature (or refrigerate in a tightly covered glass jar until ready to use).

2. Put the chicken breasts in a single layer in a shallow glass or ceramic dish; pour on the marinade; cover and marinate for at least 4 hours.

3. Prepare the grill or heat the broiler. Cook the chicken breasts 7 to 9 inches from the fire for 4 to 5 minutes on each side, basting on both sides during the cooking process.

HONEY SPICE BARBECUED CHICKEN BREASTS

4–6 servings

8 tablespoons (1 stick) butter
½ cup honey
2 tablespoons Dijon-style mustard (or other prepared mustard)
2 medium garlic cloves, crushed
¼ cup fresh lime juice
⅛ teaspoon savory
⅛ teaspoon crumbled dried rosemary
3 whole chicken breasts (about 3 pounds), halved
Salt and black pepper to taste

1. In a skillet large enough to marinate the chicken breasts, over medium-high heat, combine the butter, honey, mustard, garlic, lime juice, savory, and rosemary. Mix well. Remove the skillet from the fire.

2. Sprinkle the chicken breasts generously with salt and pepper; place in the warm marinade and leave on top of the stove for at least ½ hour.

3. Prepare the barbecue grill or heat the broiler. Remove the chicken breasts from the marinade and cook 7 to 9 inches from the fire for 4 to 5 minutes per side. Baste and turn several times during the cooking process.

Deep Frying

Successful deep frying depends on two things: The oil must be deep enough to cover each breast and hot enough to begin the cooking process *immediately*. Another important point: Never crowd the pan, as each separate piece should toss and turn gently in the hot oil . . . or boil! After the deep frying is completed, put each piece of chicken breast on a wire rack to drain for a minute. (Nothing looks or tastes worse than a puddle of grease on the bottom of a dinner plate.) Oil for deep frying should be 375° F., and no matter which recipe you chose, the chicken can be kept warm in the oven set on low for 15 to 20 minutes without losing flavor.

CRISPY HAZELNUT CHICKEN

2–4 servings

2 whole chicken breasts (about 2 pounds),
    skinned and boned
1 cup buttermilk
2 eggs, well beaten
1 cup very finely chopped blanched hazelnuts
1 cup dry bread crumbs
½ teaspoon salt
Black pepper to taste
1 teaspoon Hungarian paprika
Vegetable oil for deep frying (2 cups or more)

1. Combine the chicken breasts and the buttermilk; marinate for at least 1 hour. Drain and pat dry with paper towels. Reserve ½ cup of buttermilk.

2. Beat together the eggs and the reserved buttermilk until thoroughly combined.

3. Combine the nuts, bread crumbs, salt, pepper, and paprika. Dip the chicken breasts in the egg mixture, allowing any excess to drain off. Then coat well with the nut-crumb mixture. Refrigerate the chicken breasts for 1 hour to set. Preheat the oven to 325° F.

4. Heat the oil to about 375° F. Gently immerse the chicken breasts in the hot oil and deep fry until a golden-brown crust forms. Do this in several batches, as necessary, so the pan isn't crowded during cooking. Put the breasts in an ovenproof dish and bake for 10 minutes.

CHICKEN with BLACK WALNUTS

2–4 servings

2 whole chicken breasts (about 2 pounds),
    skinned, boned, and cut into 1 x 1-inch
    pieces
1 teaspoon salt
1 tablespoon cornstarch
1 egg white
1 tablespoon Chinese rice wine or dry sherry
2 cups plus 2 tablespoons vegetable oil
1½ cups black walnuts, blanched, drained,
    and skinned
1 green bell pepper, peeled, seeded, and
    julienned
1 red bell pepper, peeled, seeded, and
    julienned
2 tablespoons bean paste (canned—available
    in Oriental markets)
1 teaspoon sugar
2 tablespoons dry white wine
¼ cup chicken stock

1. In a bowl, combine the chicken, salt, cornstarch, egg white, and sherry; toss gently to coat completely.

2. Heat 2 cups of the oil in a wok over medium-high heat until very hot but not smoking. Put the walnuts in a strainer and immerse in the hot oil. Gently deep fry the walnuts, moving the strainer up and down so the hot fat cooks the walnuts evenly without splashing out of the wok. Cook for 2 minutes, or until golden brown; remove and drain well. Reserve the oil for cooking the chicken.

3. To a sauté pan or heavy skillet over medium-high heat, add 2 tablespoons of oil. Sauté the green and red peppers for 3 minutes, or until tender. Add the bean paste and sauté, stirring constantly, for 1 minute more.

Stir in the sugar and cook for 1 minute. Set aside.

4. Return the wok to the fire and heat the oil to very hot but not smoking. Deep fry the chicken pieces for 1 to 1½ minutes, or until golden brown. Drain them and add to the sauté pan with the peppers.

5. Over medium-high heat, add the wine to the sauté pan and cook for about 1 minute, or until the sauce thickens. Add the stock; cook for another minute or so to reduce the stock. Stir in the walnuts and toss to heat through.

CHICKEN KIEV

4 servings

8 tablespoons (1 stick) butter
2 teaspoons black pepper
2 teaspoons Hungarian sweet paprika
1 tablespoon chopped fresh parsley
4 whole chicken breasts (about 4 pounds),
    skinned, boned (do not split),
    and flattened to ⅓ inch thick
1 cup all-purpose flour for dredging
3 eggs, well beaten with ½ teaspoon salt
2 cups fresh bread crumbs
Vegetable oil for deep frying

1. In a bowl, cream together the butter, 1 teaspoon black pepper, 1 teaspoon paprika, and the parsley. Divide equally onto four pieces of waxed paper. Form into cylindrical shapes between sheets of waxed paper; freeze until very stiff, about 30 minutes.

2. Place a frozen butter cylinder in the center of each chicken breast and roll until the butter is totally enclosed. Tuck in the edges and press together to seal lightly.

3. Mix the remaining pepper and paprika with the flour. Dip each chicken roll in flour, shake off the excess, then dip it in the beaten eggs. Roll in bread crumbs. Allow to set for 5 minutes, then dip again in the eggs and roll again in bread crumbs. Refrigerate the rolls for 2 to 3 hours, covered with waxed paper or plastic wrap.

4. In a heavy skillet over medium-high heat, heat enough oil to cover the rolls. When the oil is hot enough to deep fry, place half the chicken rolls in the oil and deep fry for 4 to 5 minutes, until golden brown. Drain on several layers of paper towels. Keep warm in a low oven until all are done.

JAPANESE-STYLE CHICKEN CROQUETTES

4 servings

2 whole chicken breasts (about 2 pounds), skinned, boned, and minced
6 Japanese dried mushrooms, softened in cold water for about 15 minutes, drained, dried with paper towels, and minced
4 scallions, minced
1 egg
2 tablespoons sake
1 tablespoon light soy sauce (Japanese style)
1 teaspoon sugar
½ teaspoon salt
¼ cup dried bread crumbs
Vegetable oil for deep frying
1 cup chopped fresh parsley

1. Completely mix together the chicken, mushrooms, scallions, egg, sake, soy sauce, sugar, salt, and bread crumbs. With an oiled spoon, scoop out 1-inch balls. Roll in the palms of your hands. Place on a lightly oiled plate.

2. In a heavy skillet, heat the oil until hot enough to deep fry. The oil should be deep enough to cover the croquettes. Gently place croquettes in the pan so that they are not touching and can bob freely in the hot oil. They should begin to brown immediately. Fry in two batches, and do not crowd while deep frying.

3. Remove the croquettes from the oil with a slotted spoon and place on several layers of paper towel to drain for a minute. Roll the croquettes in chopped parsley. Arrange on a platter and serve hot.

"You can't hatch chickens from fried eggs."
Pennsylvania Dutch proverb

SPICY COUNTRY-FRIED CHICKEN BREASTS

Truly old-fashioned, Southern-style fried chicken.

4–6 servings

2 eggs, lightly beaten
½ cup buttermilk
½ teaspoon hot sauce (such as Tabasco or chili oil)
1½ cups all-purpose flour
1 tablespoon salt
1 teaspoon black pepper
½ teaspoon Hungarian hot paprika
3 whole chicken breasts (about 3 pounds), skinned (optional), boned, and halved
3 tablespoons fat rendered from 3 to 4 large pieces of bacon
Solid vegetable shortening for deep frying (3 cups or more)

1. In a bowl, thoroughly mix the eggs, buttermilk, and hot sauce. Set aside.

2. Put the flour, salt, pepper, and paprika in a brown paper bag or a large plastic bag. Hold the top of the bag tightly closed, and shake to combine the ingredients.

3. One at a time, dip the chicken breasts in the egg mixture; allow the excess to drip off; then put each piece of chicken breast in the bag and gently shake the chicken around in the flour, allowing the excess flour to fall back into the bag. Set the chicken on a plate.

4. Heat the bacon fat and shortening in a large cast iron skillet over medium-high heat. It should measure at least ½ inch deep in the skillet.

5. When the fat is hot enough to deep fry, use long-handled tongs to lower the chicken breasts into the fat, starting skin side down. Fry for about 10 minutes on each side, or until golden brown. Drain on brown paper or several layers of paper towel before serving. Serve hot or cold.

BREAD CRUMB COATING In place of flour, use 2 cups dried bread crumbs to coat the chicken. Substitute lemon juice for hot sauce, and increase the paprika to 1 teaspoon.

DEEP-FRIED CHICKEN BREAST WITH PAN GRAVY When the chicken is done, remove all but 2 tablespoons of fat from the skillet. Over medium heat, add 2 tablespoons of all-purpose flour to the fat; cook with the fat, stirring constantly, for 2 to 3 minutes to form a roux. Lower the heat and slowly add a mixture of 1 cup milk and 1 cup heavy cream to the flour and stir until smooth. Adjust seasoning with salt and pepper. Pour the sauce on a heated serving plate and arrange the chicken over it. Serve with the remaining sauce on the side.

CARIBBEAN COCONUT CHICKEN

This is another recipe that translates into finger food and hors d'oeuvres as easily as it is served for a main course.

2–4 servings

2 whole chicken breasts (about 2 pounds), skinned, boned, halved, and flattened to ¼ inch thick
4 thin slices of prosciutto
1 ripe mango, peeled and cut into 8 strips 1 inch wide
1 cup all-purpose flour
½ teaspoon salt
⅛ teaspoon black pepper
½ teaspoon curry powder
⅛ teaspoon finely crumbled dried thyme
2 eggs, well beaten
2 cups grated fresh coconut (or unsweetened shredded coconut)
Vegetable oil for deep frying (2 cups or more)
Juice of 1 fresh lime
1 to 2 limes, cut into wedges

1. Inside the edge of each pounded chicken breast, place a slice of prosciutto trimmed to ½ inch. Place a slice of mango in the center. Roll lengthwise to completely enclose the mango and prosciutto. Tuck in and pinch the ends of the chicken breasts to seal tightly. Arrange the rolls on a baking sheet and refrigerate for about 30 minutes, or until very firm.

2. In a bowl, combine the flour, salt, pepper, curry powder, and thyme. Spread the mixture on a plate. Pour the beaten eggs onto another plate. Loosely sprinkle the coconut onto a third plate.

3. When the chicken rolls are very cold and firm, roll each in the flour mixture and shake off the excess. Then roll in the beaten eggs until completely covered; drain. Finally, roll in coconut.

4. Arrange the chicken rolls on a plate in a single layer. Cover and refrigerate for 30 minutes.

5. Preheat the oven to 325° F. Heat the oil in a deep heavy skillet. The oil should be deep enough to cover the chicken rolls completely. When the oil is hot enough to deep fry, add half the chicken rolls to the skillet and deep fry until golden brown, or about 4 minutes. Remove with a slotted spoon and drain on several layers of paper towel. Repeat with the remaining chicken rolls.

6. Put the chicken rolls on a baking sheet and bake for about 10 minutes. Splash with lime juice and serve with lime wedges.

Baking

Many occasions, such as cocktail parties, gatherings after the theater, meetings at home, and large buffet dinners call for a beautifully laid table and a magnificent meal prepared in advance.

Lots of these baked chicken breast recipes can prevent you from being away from your event for longer than a few minutes. While guests are sipping a glass of wine, a spicy North African Bastille can be popped into the oven to bake, filling the room with scents reminiscent of far-off places; with the preparation done in advance, a feast fit for an Arabian Night will be ready in less than 20 minutes. Chicken Pot Pie is another recipe that fulfills these requirements beautifully.

CHICKEN BREASTS RELLENO

Many multitalented people often have a special flair for cooking. This is especially true of Gregory Lynn, who, besides being a professor of design at the University of California—Davis, is a landscape artist, an authority on palm trees, and a master over his many pots and pans. His culinary creations are always as wonderful to look at as they are to devour.

4–6 servings

4 whole chicken breasts (about 3 pounds), skinned, boned, and flattened to ¼ inch thick
⅛ teaspoon cumin
⅛ teaspoon oregano
Dash of nutmeg
1 bell pepper, seeded and quartered
slices (¼-inch-thick) Monterey Jack cheese
4 thin slices smoked or boiled ham
8 pimiento-stuffed green olives, halved
3 eggs, separated
2 tablespoons all-purpose flour
⅛ teaspoon salt
Dash of cayenne pepper
Light vegetable oil for frying
2 tablespoons chopped parsley
Lemon rounds
Green or red Mexican-style salsa (canned or bottled)

1. Starting with the bone side, sprinkle the chicken breasts with a mixture of cumin, oregano, and nutmeg. Set aside.

2. In a large saucepan filled with salted water, boil the bell pepper pieces for 4 minutes. Let cool to room temperature.

3. On half on each pounded breast, layer a piece of bell pepper, a slice of cheese, a slice of ham, and 4 olive halves. Fold over to cover all the ingredients, and seal the edges by pressing down with the tines of a fork. Preheat the oven to 350° F.

4. Lightly oil the bottom of a shallow baking dish. Arrange the chicken breasts in a single layer, cover, and bake for 6 to 8 minutes, or until they just begin to turn white. Do not overcook. Remove the pan from the oven, uncover, and allow the chicken breasts to cool.

5. Beat the egg whites until stiff and dry. In a fairly large bowl, beat the yolks well; mix in the flour, salt, and cayenne pepper. Fold a third of the egg whites into the yolk mixture. When absorbed, fold in the remaining egg whites very gently. Do not beat. The mixture should remain stiff.

6. Heat the oil (½ inch deep) in a heavy skillet to very hot but not smoking. Spoon enough egg mixture onto a saucer to cover the bottom. Place one chicken breast in the center. Spoon on enough egg mixture to cover. Remove the excess from around the edges. Slide the chicken breast into the hot oil and dry for 1 minute on each side, until golden brown and puffed. (Don't turn more than once during the cooking process.) Sprinkle with parsley, garnish with a lemon wedge, and serve salsa on the side.

TARRAGON–MUSTARD CHICKEN BREASTS

2–4 servings

2 cups dry bread crumbs
1 teaspoon salt
1 teaspoon Hungarian paprika
Black pepper to taste
1 egg
4 tablespoons Dijon-style mustard (or other prepared mustard)
2 shallots, peeled
1 tablespoon finely crushed dried tarragon leaves
8 tablespoons (1 stick) melted butter
2 whole chicken breasts (about 2 pounds), skinned, boned, and flattened slightly

Sauce
2 tablespoons Dijon-style mustard (or other prepared mustard)
2 shallots
1 teaspoon dried tarragon
¼ cup chicken stock
½ cup dry white wine
2 tablespoons (¼ stick) butter

2 teaspoons finely chopped fresh parsley

1. Preheat the oven to 375° F.

2. In a small bowl, mix together the bread crumbs, salt, paprika, and black pepper; combine well. Set aside.

3. In a blender or food processor, combine the egg, mustard, shallots, and tarragon. Add the melted butter in a thin but steady stream and blend until the mixture is light and fluffy. Put in a bowl.

4. Dip the chicken breasts in the mustard mixture, coating well. Roll in the bread crumbs. Put in a shallow ovenproof dish. Bake for 12 to 15 minutes, or just until done.

5. To prepare the sauce, in a blender combine the mustard, shallots, tarragon, stock, and wine. Put in a saucepan, bring to a boil, and reduce by half. Whisk in the butter, one tablespoon at a time. Keep warm.

6. Turn the broiler to high. Place the chicken breasts under the broiler for about 2 minutes to brown, turning once. Spoon the sauce on the bottom of individual dinner plates and place the chicken breasts on the sauce. Sprinkle with chopped parsley.

CHICKEN BREASTS with WILD MUSHROOMS

Wild mushrooms are available in gourmet food stores. Most are dried for convenient shipping.

4–6 servings

2 ounces dried wild mushrooms (such as morels, porcini, cepes, chanterelles, trompettes des morts)
8 tablespoons (1 stick) butter
2 shallots, finely minced
Dash of allspice
Salt and black pepper to taste
1 cup chicken stock, boiled to reduce to ½ cup
1 tablespoon fresh lemon juice
3 tablespoons dry sherry
1 cup heavy cream
2 tablespoons olive oil
1 large garlic clove, finely minced
3 whole chicken breasts (about 3 pounds), skinned and boned
2 tablespoons medium sherry
3 tablespoons chopped fresh parsley
2 tablespoons chopped fresh chives

1. Rehydrate the dried mushrooms and clean them well (see Note). Slice and set aside.

2. In a sauté pan or heavy skillet over medium heat, melt 6 tablespoons of the butter. Add the shallots and sauté for about 3 minutes, or until tender and lightly browned. Add the mushrooms to the sauté pan; sprinkle on the allspice and salt and pepper. Continue cooking over medium heat, stirring occasionally, for about 4 to 6 minutes, until the liquid from the mushrooms has evaporated.

3. Add to the sauté pan ¼ cup of the reduced stock, the lemon juice, and the dry sherry. Continue cooking the mushrooms until they are tender. Lower the heat, add half the cream, and simmer for 5 minutes, or until the sauce begins to thicken.

4. Lightly butter an ovenproof shallow baking dish. Spread the mushroom mixture evenly over the bottom. Set aside. Preheat the oven to 350° F.

5. In a sauté pan over medium-high heat, melt the remaining 2 tablespoons of butter with the olive oil. Sauté the garlic for about 1 minute, or until browned. Sprinkle the chicken breasts with salt and pepper to taste and sauté for about 2 to 3 minutes on each side, until lightly browned. Add the remaining ¼ cup stock and the medium sherry; continue cooking for another 2 or 3 minutes, until the liquid is reduced slightly and the chicken is almost done. Remove the chicken breasts from the pan and arrange over the mushrooms. Seal with a tight-fitting cover or foil and bake for 10 to 15 minutes.

6. Over medium heat, continue reducing the

liquid from the chicken breasts until it is almost a glaze on the bottom of the pan. Reduce the heat to low; pour in the remaining ½ cup of cream and cook until the sauce thickens, stirring constantly to incorporate all the particles from the bottom of the pan. Add the parsley. Spoon the sauce over individual servings of the chicken and mushrooms. Sprinkle with chives.

Note To rehydrate dried mushrooms, add enough boiling water to cover in a saucepan. After 2 minutes, reduce the heat to low and simmer for 20 minutes. Drain thoroughly. To clean, wipe gently with paper towels or use a soft-bristle brush to loosen dirt or sand.

CILANTRO CHICKEN SALAD

3–6 servings

3 whole chicken breasts (about 3 pounds), skinned and boned
4 tablespoons chopped fresh cilantro leaves
2 cups crème fraîche or heavy cream whipped to stiffen slightly
½ teaspoon salt, and black pepper to taste
½ cup Homemade Lemon Mayonnaise (see page 86)
½ cup sour cream
2 celery stalks, cut into 1-inch-long julienne
¾ cup very coarsely chopped black or white walnuts or toasted cashew nuts
1 cup Concord grapes, washed, halved, and seeded
¼ cup finely chopped scallions (white and some of the green part)
Assorted salad greens (Boston, Bibb, red leaf, romaine lettuce; watercress, radicchio, or other interesting salad ingredients)
4 to 6 small bunches of green or red grapes for garnish

1. Arrange the chicken breasts in a shallow heatproof pan just large enough to hold them all in a single layer. Sprinkle on 2 tablespoons of the cilantro and cover with crème fraîche. Sprinkle with salt and black pepper. Cover and marinate for at least 1 hour at room temperature.

2. Place the pan in the oven preheated to 375° F. Cover and bake the chicken breasts in the marinade for 10 to 12 minutes, or until firm to the touch. Remove the chicken breasts from the marinade, let cool, and cut into bite-size pieces.

3. Mix together the mayonnaise and sour cream.

4. Combine the celery, nuts, Concord grapes, 1 tablespoon of the cilantro, and the scallions with the chicken breast pieces; add the mayonnaise mixture and toss gently. Refrigerate for at least 2 hours. Serve on a bed of assorted greens, surrounded by bunches of grapes. Garnish with a few turns of the pepper mill. Sprinkle with remaining 1 tablespoon of cilantro.

SILVER-WRAPPED CHICKEN BREASTS

Serve this hot or cold.

2–4 servings

4 tablespoons sesame seeds
½ cup light soy sauce
2 tablespoons sugar
¼ cup sake
2 whole chicken breasts (about 2 pounds),
    skinned, boned, and quartered (to make
    a total of 8 pieces)
1 tablespoon vegetable oil
¼ teaspoon black pepper
4 scallions (white and some of the green
    part), chopped
8 very thin round lemon slices

1. In a heavy skillet over medium high heat, toast the sesame seeds until they turn brown and start to popu. Remove from the heat and set aside to cool.

2. Combine the soy sauce, sugar, and sake in a bowl. Add the chicken breasts. Cover and marinate for at least 30 minutes. Preheat the oven to 350° F.

3. Measure out 8 pieces of aluminum foil large enough to make a loose package around each piece of chicken breast. Lightly brush each piece of foil with oil.

4. Remove the chicken breasts from the marinade and put each piece on foil. (There should be some liquid still on the chicken breasts.) Sprinkle with black pepper, sesame seeds, and scallions.

5. Wrap the foil loosely around the chicken breast pieces, making sure to seal tightly so the moisture does not escape during cooking. Put the foil package on a baking sheet and bake for 20 to 25 minutes.

ALMOND CHICKEN BREASTS

From Rosemary Gelbach, who says this recipe is very rich—great for special occasions.

4–6 servings

2 eggs, lightly beaten
½ cup half-and-half
½ cup milk
1 teaspoon salt
1 teaspoon Hungarian paprika
¾ cup all-purpose flour
3 whole chicken breasts (about 3 pounds),
    skinned, boned, and flattened to ⅓ inch
All-purpose flour for dredging
1 cup ground blanched almonds
½ cup dried bread crumbs
8 tablespoons (1 stick) butter
¼ cup sliced almonds
2 tablespoons melted butter

1. Fifteen to 30 minutes before you're ready to bake, preheat the oven to 350° F. Lightly butter the bottom of an ovenproof baking dish.

2. In a bowl, combine the eggs, half-and-half, milk, salt, paprika, and flour; beat to form a pasty batter. Marinate the chicken breasts in the batter for at least an hour in the refrigerator.

3. Combine the ground almonds and bread crumbs; spread evenly over a sheet of waxed paper.

4. Remove the chicken breasts from the marinade; drain. Coat with bread crumbs. Allow to set for 15 minutes.

5. In a heavy skillet or sauté pan over medium heat, melt the butter. Add the chicken breasts and cook for about 2 to 3 minutes on each side, until lightly browned. Place in the prepared baking dish, sprinkle with sliced almonds, drizzle with melted butter and bake for 15 minutes, or until crisp and golden brown.

GLAZED CHICKEN BREASTS

2–4 servings

1 tablespoon melted butter
1 whole chicken breasts (about 2 pounds), halved

Mango Chutney Glaze
1 garlic clove
Salt and black pepper to taste
2 tablespoons (¼ stick) butter
½ cup finely chopped Major Grey's mango chutney

Apricot Mustard Glaze
½ cup apricot preserves
1 tablespoon prepared mustard (Dijon-style or other French mustard)
2 tablespoons (¼ stick) butter
Salt and white pepper to taste

1 to 2 teaspoons fresh lemon juice

1. Preheat the oven to 350° F. Coat the bottom of a shallow baking dish with melted butter.

2. Put the chicken breasts, skin side down, in the pan. Bake for 10 minutes.

3. Combine the ingredients for the glaze of your choice in a blender and mix thoroughly.

4. Remove the pan from the oven, turn the chicken breasts, and coat with the glaze. Return to the oven for 10 minutes, or until done.

5. Drizzle lemon juice over each piece of glazed chicken breast.

CHICKEN POT PIE

Some might say the origin of chicken pot pie is English. This one, however, originated in the kitchen of Barbara Gorin, a private chef who lives and works in New York City. Along with her seafood sausage, chopped salads, and Grand Marnier soufflés, this divinely delicious pot pie, made with a rich chicken breast filling and a lighter-than-air pastry top, has been eagerly consumed by a mayor, some chairmen of the board, a socialite or two—and now you can share the delights with friends and family.

6–8 servings

Stock
Bones from 5 whole chicken breasts
1 celery stalk
1 carrot, chopped
1 medium onion, quartered
1 tablespoon salt
10 whole black peppercorns
5 whole cloves
5 sprigs of fresh parsley
1 large bay leaf

Pastry
1 cup all-purpose flour
1 teaspoon baking powder
½ teaspoon salt
4 tablespoons (½ stick) cold butter
1 ½ tablespoons lard
⅓ cup ice cold water

Filling
Meat from 5 whole chicken breasts (about 5 pounds), cut into bite-size pieces
Flour for dredging
Vegetable oil for frying
Salt and black pepper to taste
Herbes de Provence

Sauce
6 tablespoons (¾ stick) butter
7 tablespoons all-purpose flour
3 cups warm stock
½ cup heavy cream
Salt and black pepper to taste
Dash of mace

Pastry Glaze
1 egg mixed with 1 tablespoon water

1. Simmer all the stock ingredients in water to cover for 1 hour. Let cool and strain. Set aside.

2. To make the crust, in a large bowl combine the flour, baking powder, and salt. Using a pastry cutter or two knives, cut in the butter and lard to form pieces about the size of rice. Add the ice water all at once, and stir quickly with a fork just until mixed. Refrigerate, covered, for 1 to 2 hours.

3. Coat the chicken breast pieces with flour. Heat just enough oil to cover the bottom of a 12- to 14-inch heavy skillet over medium-high heat. Sear the chicken until lightly browned; remove and sprinkle with salt, black pepper, and herbes de Provence. Set aside.

4. To make the sauce, melt the butter in a 4-quart saucepan over low heat. Stirring constantly, add the flour and cook to form a roux (mixture should be slightly browned). Continue stirring and slowly add the stock. Cook the mixture over low heat until it thickens. Stir in the cream. Add salt, pepper, and mace to taste. Combine the chicken with the sauce and put the mixture in an ovenproof casserole dish. Preheat the oven to 350° F.

5. On a lightly floured board or pastry cloth, roll out the pastry to ⅛ inch thick. Shape the pastry to match the casserole dish and carefully transfer the pastry to the top of the chicken breast mixture; cover completely. Tuck any overlapping pastry into the casserole. Decorate the top with pastry scraps cut into leaf shapes. Cut a slit in the middle of the pastry to allow the steam to escape during cooking.

6. Brush the pastry with the egg glaze. Bake for 35 to 45 minutes, or until the crust is golden and the filling is bubbling hot.

CHICKEN BREASTS with GREEN CHILIES

2–4 servings

4 tablespoons vegetable oil
2 whole chicken breasts (about 2 pounds), halved
1 cup minced onion
20 mild green chilies (canned or bottled from California)
1½ cups heavy cream
1 teaspoon Tabasco sauce
2 teaspoons fresh lemon juice
½ teaspoon salt
Black pepper to taste
1 cup grated Monterey Jack cheese

1. Heat the oil in a sauté pan or heavy skillet over medium-high heat. Sauté the chicken breasts about 2 to 3 minutes, or until lightly browned, on the skin side only. Put them in a single layer in an ovenproof casserole, skin side up.

2. Add the onion to the sauté pan and cook until translucent. Add half the chilies, heat through, and pour the mixture over the chicken breasts. Preheat the oven to 350° F.

3. In a blender or food processor, combine the remaining chilies, cream, Tabasco sauce, lemon juice, salt, and black pepper; combine until slightly thickened. Pour over the chicken and sprinkle on the cheese.

4. Bake for 30 minutes.

BASTILLE

From Donna Adams, a cooking teacher in Cleveland.

4–6 servings

4 tablespoons (½ stick) butter
1 cup chicken stock
1 teaspoon curry powder
1 onion, finely chopped
1 sprig of fresh coriander
1 teaspoon ground ginger
¼ teaspoon cinnamon
Pinch of allspice
1 tablespoon chopped parsley
2 whole chicken breasts (about 2 pounds)
¾ cup finely chopped blanched almonds
2 tablespoons sugar
1 tablespoon lemon juice
4 eggs, lightly beaten
8 sheets phyllo dough
8 tablespoons (1 stick) melted butter
Powdered sugar
Cinnamon

1. In a small saucepan, combine 2 tablespoons of the butter, the stock, curry powder, onion, coriander, ginger, cinnamon, allspice, and parsley; bring to a boil. Reduce the heat to medium and continue cooking, uncovered, for 15 minutes.

2. Add the chicken breasts to the saucepan, cover, and simmer for 10 minutes, or until firm to the touch. Let cool to room temperature. Remove the chicken breasts; reserve the stock in its saucepan. Discard the bones and skin; cut the meat into small bite-size pieces. Set the chicken aside.

3. In a small sauté pan over medium heat, melt the 2 remaining tablespoons of butter. Sauté the almonds for 2 to 3 minutes, or until lightly browned. Remove from the heat and add the sugar. Stir and set aside.

4. Place the reserved liquid over medium heat. Add the lemon juice and bring to a simmer. Add the eggs, cooking until done. (This mixture will be somewhat curdled and have the appearance of scrambled eggs.) Remove from the heat and set aside.

5. Brush a lightly dampened dish towel (not terry cloth) with melted butter and on it place a sheet of phyllo dough. Coat generously with melted butter. Continue layering all the sheets of the phyllo dough, brushing each with a generous amount of melted butter before topping with the next.

6. Layer the chicken mixture, the egg, and

then the nut mixture over the phyllo dough; spread evenly. Carefully roll up the dough, like a jelly roll. Place in a shallow baking pan seam side down brushed with melted butter on the bottom; tuck the ends under. Cover with the dampened dish towel until you are ready to bake.

7. Fifteen to 30 minutes before you are ready to bake the Bastille, preheat the oven to 425° F. Bake the Bastille for 25 to 30 minutes. When done, sprinkle generously with powdered sugar and a small amount of cinnamon. Let cool slightly, and slice just before serving. Serve hot or warm.

CHICKEN BAKED IN CLAY

Clay-pot cooking is quick and versatile, and just about any ingredients put in the pot will taste terrific with chicken breasts once the flavors "get together." Remember, always put the tightly closed clay pot in a cold oven, then turn on the heat. The clay could crack if put in a hot oven.

2–4 servings

2 whole chicken breasts (about 2 pounds), skinned and boned (optional)
4 tablespoons (½ stick) butter, cut into pieces
¼ teaspoon dried oregano
1 teaspoon chopped fresh basil (or ½ teaspoon dried)
3 garlic cloves, peeled and minced
Salt and black pepper
¼ cup chicken stock
½ cup dry sherry, vermouth, or white wine
2 green apples, cored and sliced

1. Put the chicken breasts in a clay pot, bone side up. Dot with butter; sprinkle with oregano or basil, garlic, and salt and pepper.

2. Warm the stock and wine slightly. Pour over the chicken pieces. Arrange the apple slices around the chicken breasts. Close the clay pot tightly. Place in the center of the cold oven, directly on the oven rack. Close the door and turn the heat to 450° F. Bake 40 to 45 minutes, or until the chicken is very tender.

GREEK CHICKEN BREASTS Rub the chicken breasts with garlic and olive oil and sprinkle with salt, pepper, and oregano. Make a layer of thinly sliced lemon rounds on the bottom of the clay pot. Put the chicken breasts on the lemon and surround with Greek olives. Bake as directed.

ORANGE CHICKEN BREASTS BAKED IN CLAY Put ½ cup slightly warmed orange juice, 2 medium onions, quartered, 1 teaspoon fine herbes, 4 tablespoons butter, ½ teaspoon white pepper, salt to taste, 1 teaspoon dill, and 2 tablespoons Cointreau (orange liqueur) in the clay pot along with the chicken breasts, breast side down. Seal and bake as directed.

CHICKEN BREASTS PARMESAN

2–4 servings

½ cup all-purpose flour
2 whole chicken breasts (about 2 pounds),
    skinned, boned, halved, and flattened to
    ½ inch thick
½ teaspoon salt
¼ teaspoon white pepper
2 eggs, well beaten
1 cup freshly grated Parmesan cheese (or
    more to taste)
8 tablespoons (1 stick) butter
¼ cup finely chopped fresh parsley

1. Put the flour on a plate. Dredge the chicken breasts in it and shake off the excess.

2. Sprinkle the chicken breasts with salt and pepper.

3. In a bowl, beat the eggs into the Parmesan cheese, making a stiff batter. Dip the breasts in the batter until well coated. Allow to stand at room temperature for about 1 hour to set.

4. Preheat the oven to 325° F. In a heavy skillet or sauté pan over medium heat, melt the butter. Sauté the chicken breasts for 2 to 3 minutes on each side, or until the batter is golden brown.

5. Place in an ovenproof dish in a single layer; bake for 10 to 12 minutes. Sprinkle with chopped parsley before serving.

CHICKEN BREASTS with CHICKEN LIVER STUFFING

6 tablespoons (¾ stick) butter
2 tablespoons pine nuts
¼ pound chicken livers
1 garlic clove, minced
2 tablespoons finely chopped shallots
2 tablespoons minced fresh parsley
Pinch of nutmeg
Salt and black pepper to taste
4 tablespoons dry white wine
4 large springs of parsley for garnish

2 whole chicken breasts (about 2 pounds),
    skinned, boned, and prepared
    for stuffing (see page 00)
3 tablespoons melted butter

1. In a sauté pan or heavy skillet over medium heat, melt 2 tablespons of the butter. Sauté the pine nuts until browned. Remove from the pan and set aside to cool.

2. In the same sauté pan over medium heat, melt an additional 2 tablespoons of butter. Sauté the chicken livers for about 3 to 4 minutes, so they are still pink inside. Set aside.

3. Add the garlic to the sauté pan and cook 1 minute, or until browned. Turn the heat up to medium-high and sauté the shallots until soft. Add the minced parsley, nutmeg, salt and pepper, and 2 tablespoons of the wine and continue sautéing about 2 minutes, or until the wine has evaporated completely. Remove from the heat and let cool slightly.

4. Coarsely chop the pine nuts. Mash the chicken livers with the tines of a fork to form a paste. Combine the chicken livers with the parsley and shallot mixture; fold in the pine nuts. Place equal amounts of the stuffing in each prepared chicken breast. Press the edges together to seal.

5. Preheat the oven to 325° F.

6. In a sauté pan over medium-high heat, melt the remaining 2 tablespoons of butter. Sauté the chicken breasts for 2 to 3 minutes on each side, or just until lightly browned. When turning the breasts, be very careful that the stuffing does not come out. Transfer the chicken breasts to an overproof baking pan.

7. To the sauté pan, over high heat, add the remaining 2 tablespoons of wine; stir while reducing slightly, and pour over the chicken breasts. Cover the pan tightly with foil and bake for 10 to 12 minutes, or until done. Transfer to a serving platter and garnish with parsley.

ITALIAN SAUSAGE STUFFING In a sauté pan over medium heat, melt 2 tablespoons butter. Add ¼ pound finely ground Italian sausage meat, cooking until almost done. Add ¼ cup finely chopped onion, and continue sautéing until the onion is tender; add black pepper to taste, and ¼ teaspoon dried oregano. Combine ½ cup fresh bread crumbs, ¼ cup chopped parsley, and salt to taste. Mix into the sausage. Stuff the chicken breasts and bake as directed.

SPINACH AND FETA STUFFING In a sauté pan over medium heat, melt 2 tablespoons unsalted butter. Add ¼ teaspoon dried oregano, ⅛ teaspoon salt, and ½ cup finely chopped onions, and continue cooking until the onions are translucent. Add ¼ pound washed and chopped fresh spinach leaves and 2 tablespoons coarsely chopped walnuts. Cook 3 minutes more. Remove the pan from the heat and cool slightly. Stir in ¼ cup of crumbled feta. Stuff the chicken breasts, and bake as directed.

HOW TO STUFF CHICKEN BREASTS

Chicken breasts conveniently become tasty envelopes for almost any type of stuffing. Since the pocket is small, stuffings with intense flavorings are best.

Put a skinned and boned chicken breast in the freezer for 30 minutes. Remove it to a work surface, skin side up. Insert the tip of a sharp boning knife into the thickest part of the breast. Make a slit in the meat that runs about three quarters the length of the breast and about 1 inch to 1½ inches deep. Stuff with your choice of filling, and press the edges together to seal.

ACAPULCO ENCHILADA

2–4 servings

3 cups shredded poached chicken breasts
½ cup minced scallions (white and some of
    the green part)
½ cup chopped blanched almonds
½ teaspoon salt
3 cups Enchilada Chili Sauce (recipe follows)
8 uncooked flat corn tortillas (must be very
    fresh)
¾ cup sour cream
½ cup shredded Cheddar cheese
½ cup sliced pitted ripe olives
Additional sour cream and scallions to serve
    on the side

Enchilada Chili Sauce
2 tablespoons vegetable oil
⅔ cup chopped onion
¼ cup chopped green bell pepper
1 garlic clove, minced
1 cup tomato paste
1 cup water
¼ cup chili powder
1 teaspoon salt
½ teaspoon dried oregano

1. In a small bowl, toss together the shredded chicken, scallions, and almonds. Sprinkle on the salt, mix, and set aside.

2. To prepare the chili sauce heat the oil in a sauté pan over medium-high heat; add the onion, bell pepper, and garlic and sauté until the vegetables are soft. Stir in the tomato paste, water, chili powder, salt, and oregano, blending well. Lower the heat, cover, and simmer for 5 minutes.

3. Preheat the oven to 350° F.

4. To assemble the enchiladas, lightly oil the bottom of a shallow ovenproof casserole. (Decorative Mexican pottery is especially nice for serving.) Dip a tortilla in the hot sauce until partially saturated. Then place the tortilla in the casserole dish; fill with one eighth of the chicken mixture, and top with 1 tablespoon of sour cream; roll into an enchilada, seam side down. Repeat with the remaining tortillas. When the casserole is filled, drizzle the remaining sauce over the enchiladas, sprinkle with Cheddar cheese, and top with olives.

5. Bake the enchiladas for 15 minutes, or until the cheese and sauce are hot and bubbling. Serve with additional sour cream and chopped scallions on the side.

SPICY INDIAN CHICKEN BREASTS

3–6 servings

3 whole chicken breasts (about 3 pounds),
    halved
¼ teaspoon powdered mustard
1 teaspoon water
½ teaspoon crushed red pepper flakes
½ teaspoon freshly ground black pepper
½ teaspoon ground cardamom
½ teaspoon ground ginger
½ teaspoon cumin seed
1 teaspoon curry powder
2 garlic cloves, peeled
1 tablespoon salt
¼ cup cider vinegar
2 tablespoons fresh lemon juice
2 cups plain yogurt
½ cup vegetable oil

1. Arrange the chicken breasts in a single layer in a shallow glass or ceramic dish.

2. In a food processor or blender, combine the mustard, water, red pepper, black pepper, cardamon, ginger, cumin, curry powder, garlic, salt, vinegar, lemon juice, and yogurt; blend thoroughly.

3. Pour the mixture over the chicken; refrigerate, covered, for 12 hours.

4. Preheat the oven to 325° F. when you are ready to cook the chicken breasts. In a sauté pan or heavy skillet, heat the oil. Remove the chicken breasts from the yogurt mixture, letting the excess marinade drain back into the dish. Reserve the marinade.

5. Sauté the chicken breasts for 2 to 3 minutes on each side, or just until lightly browned. Do not overcook. Arrange the chicken breasts in an ovenproof casserole and pour the reserved marinade over the chicken. Bake, uncovered, for 1 hour, basting as needed.

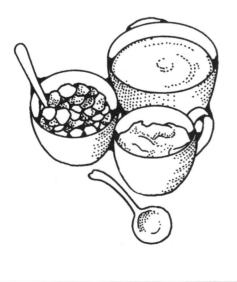

APRICOT-ALMOND CHICKEN BREAST PAUPIETTES

From Ronnie Tandler, owner and chef of Foodart Catering Service, Soho, New York City.

4–6 servings

4 garlic cloves, peeled
1 cup finely chopped dried apricots,
    marinated in 1 cup apple juice until soft
    (reserve ½ cup of the apple juice)
½ cup finely minced fresh parsley
Salt and white pepper to taste
4 tablespoons olive oil
3 whole chicken breasts (about 3 pounds),
    skinned, boned, halved, and clattered to
    ¼ inch thick
½ cup white raisins
1 cup sour cream
¼ cup sliced almonds, toasted in a 350° F.
    oven for 10 minutes, until brown and
    crispy

1. Preheat the oven to 350° F. Lightly oil the bottom of a 7 x 11-inch baking pan.

2. In a food procesor or blender, make a paste of the garlic, softened apricots, parsley, and salt and pepper.

3. Heat the oil in a sauté pan over medium-low heat. Add the apricot mixture and cook for about 5 minutes, stirring constantly.

4. Spread half the mixture on the flattened chicken breasts, roll into paupiettes (like jelly roll), and place, seam side down, in the baking pan. Tent the pan with foil. Bake for 12 to 15 minutes, or just until done. Do not overbake.

5. To make the sauce, put the reserved apple juice and the raisins in the sauté pan over medium-high heat. Increase the heat and cook until the liquid has almost completely evaporated. Remove the pan from the heat; stir in the sour cream until thoroughly blended. Return to *very* low heat, just to warm through. Pour the sauce over the paupiettes and sprinkle with toasted almonds.

WALNUT AND GARLIC BAKED PAUPIETTES OF CHICKEN BREAST In place of the apricots, use 1 cup walnuts, and walnut oil instead of olive oil. Eliminate the raisins. Prepare in the same way and cook as directed.

Poaching

Poaching—this most favorable of cooking techniques—should never be confused with boiling. Simmering liquid slowly cooks the chicken breast in this delicate process, and, if done with patience, poaching renders the chicken breast extraordinarily tender and flavorful as the herbs and spices or other essences are absorbed.

Chicken breasts can be poached in a variety of liquids, including water, wine, juice, and stock.

To poach chicken breasts in a large saucepan or stockpot, bring the poaching liquid to a boil. Add the chicken breasts and arrange them in a single layer; add any other ingredients called for by the recipe. Lower the heat, cover, and simmer for 8 to 10 minutes, or just until the chicken breasts are firm to the touch. Remove the pan from the heat and uncover it. Let the chicken breasts cool in the poaching liquid. Discard the skin, bones, and poaching liquid.

CHICKEN BREAST SKEWERS with RICE SALAD

3–6 servings

3 whole chicken breasts (about 3 pounds), skinned, boned, and quartered
12 cherry tomatoes
1 bell pepper and 1 sweet red pepper, seeded and cut into eighths lengthwise
12 small mushrooms, washed
8 pearl onions, peeled
2 cups dry white wine
2 cups chicken stock
1 bouquet garni (see page 11), including at least 2 sprigs of parsley

Rice Salad

6 cups cooked white rice, at room temperature
4 scallions (white and most of the green part), chopped
1 tablespoon finely chopped fresh mint
2 tablespoons coarsely chopped flat-leaved parsley
½ cup white raisins, soaked in 1 tablespoon dry sherry for 30 minutes
½ cup coarsely chopped pecans

Vinaigrette

1 cup olive oil
⅓ cup Champagne or white wine vinegar
Salt and black pepper to taste
1 tablespoon Dijon-style mustard or 1½ teaspoons fresh lemon juice
½ teaspoon sugar

2 bunches of watercress, washed

1. To assemble the chicken breasts and vegetables, use 4 8-inch-long wooden skewers. Divide the chicken and vegetables into equal amounts; arrange, alternating chicken breast pieces and vegetables on the skewers.

2. In a large saucepan or stockpot, bring the wine and stock to a boil. Add the skewers and arrange in a single layer; add the bouquet garni, cover, and lower the heat. Simmer the skewers for 6 to 8 minutes, or until the chicken pieces are firm to the touch. Remove from the heat, uncover, and let cool in the stock for 5 minutes, no more. Place on a platter and refrigerate for 1 hour or more. (The skewers can be served cold or at room temperature.)

3. To make the rice salad, combine all the salad ingredients in a large glass or ceramic bowl; toss to mix thoroughly.

4. Combine the vinaigrette ingredients in a jar; cover tightly and shake vigorously. Pour half the salad dressing over the rice mixture and toss to combine.

5. Place the watercress around the edges of a large serving platter. With the remaining watercress, make a line (or fencelike separation) in the center of the platter. On one side, stack the skewers. On the other, put the rice salad. Serve some watercress along with each serving of rice salad and chicken breast skewer. Serve the remaining dressing on the side.

DRUNKEN CHICKEN SALAD

3–6 servings

3 cups chicken stock
2 whole chicken breasts (about 2 pounds), halved
4 scallions, chopped (white and green parts)
1 cup Chinese rice wine or medium sherry (or a combination of both)
1 teaspoon salt
½ teaspoon sugar
1 bunch fresh coriander leaves, stems removed
3 tablespoons sesame seeds, toasted until golden brown

1. In a large saucepan or stockpot, bring the stock to a boil; add the chicken breasts, arrange in a single layer, and add half of the scallions. Reduce the heat to low, cover, and poach for 8 to 10 minutes, or until the chicken breasts are firm to the touch. Remove the pan from the heat, uncover, and let the chicken cool in the stock. Remove and discard the skin, bones, and stock. Cut the breasts into quarters and put in a large bowl with the wine, salt, and sugar. Toss, cover, and marinate for 24 hours in the refrigerator.

2. Drain off the marinade. Arrange the coriander leaves on a serving platter; place the chicken pieces in the center, and sprinkle with sesame seeds and the remaining scallions.

CURRIED CHICKEN SALAD

2–4 servings

3 cups chicken stock
2 whole chicken breasts (about 2 pounds), halved
½ cup Homemade Lemon Mayonnaise (see page 86)
½ cup white raisins
½ cup sliced almonds
¾ teaspoon white pepper
2 tablespoons curry powder
½ cup well-chopped Major Grey's chutney
2 teaspoons fresh lemon juice

1. In a large saucepan or stockpot, bring the stock to a boil. Add the chicken breasts, arrange in a single layer and cover. Lower the heat and simmer for 8 to 10 minutes, or until firm. Remove from the heat, uncover, and let cool to room temperature. Remove the bones and skin. Discard along with the stock. Cut the chicken breasts into bite-size pieces and refrigerate for about 1 hour, or until cold.

2. Make the mayonnaise; set aside. Gently toss together chicken breast pieces, raisins, almonds, white pepper, curry powder, and chutney. Add the mayonnaise, combine thoroughly, and refrigerate. Serve cold, sprinkled with a few drops of lemon juice.

SAUCES TO SERVE WITH COLD POACHED CHICKEN BREASTS

Dill and Mustard Sauce

6 tablespoons spicy brown mustard
2 tablespoons Dijon-style mustard
3 tablespoons white wine vinegar
1 tablespoon sugar
Salt and pepper to taste
½ cup light vegetable oil
½ cup chopped fresh dill

1. In a bowl, combine both mustards, vinegar, sugar, and salt and pepper. Whisk in the oil, beating constantly until smooth and well blended.

2. Stir in the dill. If you're not using the sauce immediately, whisk again before serving. Drizzle over cold poached chicken breasts or place a dollop on the side of the plate.

Fresh Tarragon Sauce

3 tablespoons tarragon wine vinegar
2 tablespoons minced fresh tarragon leaves
2 teaspoons Dijon-style mustard
Salt and pepper to taste
¾ cup olive oil

1. In a bowl, combine the vinegar, tarragon, mustard, and salt and pepper. Whisk in the olive oil, beating until thoroughly combined.

2. In a shallow glass dish, combine the sauce with 1 to 1 ½ pounds cold poached chicken breast strips, marinated in the refrigerator for at least 1 hour before serving. Remove the chicken from the sauce and arrange on a platter; whisk the sauce until well mixed and drizzle over the chicken breast strips, or serve in a dish on the side.

Sweet Curry Sauce

2 cups sour cream (or 1 cup sour cream and 1 cup plain yogurt)
1 garlic clove, minced
2 tablespoons curry powder
3 tablespoons olive oil
2 teaspoons sugar
Juice of 2 medium oranges
2 tablespoons fresh lemon juice
2 tablespoons chopped fruit chutney (such as Major Grey's mango chutney; peach, apple-spice chutney, etc.)
Salt and black pepper to taste
1 ounce gin

1. Put the sour cream in a small bowl.

2. In a saucepan over very low heat, cook the garlic and curry powder in the olive oil. Remove from the heat and stir into the sour cream. Add the sugar, orange and lemon juice, chutney, and salt and pepper; stir until well combined.

3. Transfer the mixture to a bowl, cover, and refrigerate. Just before you are ready to spoon over cold poached chicken breasts, stir in the gin.

Creamy Horseradish Sauce

1 ½ cups sour cream
1 ½ cups Homemade Lemon Mayonnaise
    (see page 86)
4 tablespoons fresh lemon juice
1 teaspoon grated lemon zest
1 ½ tablespoons white horseradish
Salt to taste

Combine all the ingredients in a covered
bowl and refrigerate until ready to serve.
Whisk to aerate.

Lemon Anchovy Sauce

2 egg yolks
3 tablespoons Dijon-style mustard
1 2-ounce can of anchovies, soaked in water
    for 30 minutes, drained, and dried
Juice of 1 lemon
1 shallot, peeled and chopped
1 cup light vegetable oil
¼ cup crème fraîche (see page 11) or sour
    cream
Salt and black pepper to taste

1. In a food processor or blender, combine
the egg yolks and mustard. When smooth,
drop in the anchovies. Blend in the lemon
juice and shallot. Continue blending until the
mixture is light and foamy.

2. Leaving the machine running, drizzle in
the oil until thoroughly incorporated. Remove the mixture from the food processor
and fold into the cream. Season with salt and
pepper. Refrigerate until ready to serve.

Fresh Tomato Vinaigrette Sauce

1 shallot, minced
⅓ cup sherry wine vinegar
2 sprigs fresh tarragon leaves
1 tablespoon tomato paste
¼ cup water
1 large ripe tomato, peeled, seeded, and
    diced
½ cup olive oil
2 cups tomato juice (unsalted)
1 teaspoon salt
½ teaspoon black pepper

1. In a small saucepan over medium-high
heat, combine the shallot, vinegar, tarragon,
tomato paste, and water. Cook until the mixture is reduced to one third of the original
amount. Let cool to room temperature.

2. Put the cooled mixture in a blender or food
processor. Add the tomato and process until
very smooth.

3. With the machine running, drizzle in the
olive oil. Add the tomato juice and blend
thoroughly. Season with salt and pepper. Refrigerate until well chilled. Whisk before
serving.

Yogurt Dressing (Especially low-calorie)
1½ cups plain yogurt
2 teaspoons chopped fresh dill
1 teaspoon salt
1 teaspoon white pepper
1 tablespoon sugar
2 tablespoons light vegetable oil
Juice of 2 lemons
2 tablespoons herb-flavored vinegar
1 cucumber, seeded and coarsely chopped
4 scallions, seeded and coarsely chopped

1. Put all the ingredients, except scallions and cucumber, in a blender. Combine thoroughly and remove to a bowl.

2. Fold in the cucumber and sprinkle with scallions.

3. Serve spooned over cold poached chicken breasts or on the side as a dipping sauce.

Homemade Lemon Mayonnaise
1 whole egg plus 2 egg yolks
½ cup fresh lemon juice
Salt and white pepper to taste
2¼ cups olive oil (pure virgin oil only)

1. In a blender or food processor bowl, combine the egg, yolks, lemon juice, and salt and pepper. Mix well.

2. With the motor running, pour in the olive oil in a small but steady stream until thoroughly incorporated. Taste for seasoning. Refrigerate in a glass jar until ready to use.

CHICKEN, AVOCADO, AND WILD RICE SALAD

2–4 servings

3 cups cooked wild rice
1 large or two medium-size ripe avocados
1 tablespoon fresh lemon juice
4 scallions (white and some of the green part), coarsely chopped
12 pitted black olives, sliced
3 cups bite-size pieces of cold poached chicken breast (see page 81), cubed

Dressing
¼ cup red wine vinegar
2 teaspoons Dijon-style mustard
½ cup light vegetable oil
½ teaspoon sugar
1 tablespoon chopped fresh parsley

¼ cup slivered almonds or toasted pine nuts for garnish
12 cherry tomatoes for garnish

1. Refrigerate the wild rice until cold.

2. Peel the avocado and slice lengthwise into ½-inch-thick strips. Coat with lemon juice, and refrigerate until well chilled.

3. In a large mixing bowl, combine the scallions, olives, chicken, and rice. Toss gently just until mixed.

4. In a small bowl, mix the vinegar, mustard, vegetable oil, sugar, and parsley. Whisk together vigorously until completely combined.

5. Just before serving, add the avocado slices to the chicken and rice mixture. Pour on the dressing and toss gently to combine thoroughly. Serve sprinkled with toasted nuts and cherry tomatoes.

CHICKEN, PASTA, AND ARTICHOKE SALAD

4–6 servings

3 cups bite-size pieces of poached chicken
    breast (see page 81)
1 ½ cups quartered artichoke hearts
½ cup broccoli florets, cooked until crisp-
    tender and drained
4 scallions (white and green parts), cut into
    ¼ -inch pieces
Salt and black pepper to taste

Basil Cream Dressing
¼ cup white wine vinegar
2 tablespoons Dijon-style mustard
1 egg yolk
2 garlic cloves, peeled
⅓ cup light vegetable oil
1 ½ cups sour cream
½ cup tightly packed chopped fresh basil
    leaves
Salt and a generous amount of black pepper

½ pound pasta shells, cooked until *al dente,*
    rinsed and drained
2 tablespoons chopped fresh chives

1. Combine the chicken breast pieces, artichoke hearts, broccoli, scallions, and salt and pepper. Refrigerate until well chilled.

2. To prepare the dressing, combine the vinegar, mustard, egg yolk, and garlic in a food processor or blender. Blend until smooth. Leave the machine running and pour in the oil in a slow but steady stream. Add the sour cream and blend thoroughly. Remove to a bowl and fold in the chopped basil and salt and pepper. Refrigerate for at least 1 hour before serving.

3. When ready to serve the salad, combine the chicken breast mixture with the pasta shells. Drizzle on the dressing and toss gently. Garnish with chives.

COLD POACHED LIME AND BASIL CHICKEN BREASTS

This is a recipe that lends itself beautifully to serving at buffet for lots of guests. Its creator, Jack Leutza of San Francisco, suggests quadrupling the ingredients and inviting twenty for a summer buffet. In fact, Jack added this little note at the bottom of the page when he sent the recipe to me: "Darling, it's a guaranteed elegant showstopper which has spread my reputation as a cook significantly."

2–4 servings

3 cups chicken stock
2 whole chicken breasts (about 2 pounds), halved

Marinade
½ cup fresh lime juice (about 4 large limes)
2 large garlic cloves, peeled and crushed
2 tablespoons packed fresh basil (or 1 tablespoon crushed dried)
2 large shallots, minced
½ cup olive oil
⅓ cup light vegetable oil
¾ teaspoon sugar
½ teaspoon salt
1 teaspoon black pepper, or to taste

Assorted salad greens

1. In a large saucepan or stockpot, bring the stock to a boil. Add the chicken breasts and arrange in a single layer. Lower the heat, cover, and simmer for 8 to 10 minutes, or until firm to the touch. Remove from the heat and let the chicken breasts cool in the stock. Remove and discard the skin, bones, and stock.

2. In a small bowl, combine the lime juice, garlic, basil, shallots, olive and vegetable oil, sugar, salt, and pepper.

3. Slice the chicken breasts into ½-inch-wide strips; put in a shallow glass dish and pour in the marinade. Cover and marinate in the refrigerator for 24 hours.

4. Drain off the marinade, put the chicken strips on a bed of salad greens, and surround with assorted salad greens.

"A good meal ought to begin with hunger."
French proverb

MANDARIN ORANGE CHICKEN SALAD

2–4 servings

3 cups orange juice
2 whole chicken breasts (about 2 pounds),
  halved
6 to 8 pitted fresh dates, chopped
¼ cup coarsely chopped blanched almonds
1 cup canned mandarin orange segments,
  drained (reserve ⅓ cup syrup)
4 scallions, julienned lengthwise into 1-inch
  strips
½ cup fresh peas, blanched
2 teaspoons fresh lemon juice
Assorted salad greens (Boston, Bibb, red leaf
  lettuce, romaine)

Cinnamon Vinaigrette

⅓ cup juice from canned mandarin orange
  segments
3 tablespoons olive oil
3 tablespoon light vegetable oil
3 tablespoons Champagne or white wine
  vinegar
Salt and white pepper to taste
2 teaspoons ground cinnamon

1. In a large saucepan or stockpot, bring the orange juice to a boil. Add the chicken breasts, arranged in a single layer. Cover and lower the heat. Simmer for 8 to 10 minutes, or until the breasts are firm. Remove from the heat, uncover, and let cool to room temperature in the orange juice.

2. Remove the skin and bones; discard. Cut the chicken into 1-inch strips. Refrigerate until cold.

3. In a large bowl, combine the chicken, dates, almonds, mandarin oranges, scallions, fresh peas and lemon juice. Toss gently. Arrange the salad greens on a large platter.

4. To prepare the cinnamon vinaigrette, combine the mandarin orange syrup, olive and vegetable oil, vinegar, salt and pepper, and cinnamon; whisk until thoroughly mixed. Immediately pour over the chicken breast mixture, and toss gently until mixture is thoroughly covered with vinaigrette. Place in the center of the salad platter. Refrigerate until ready to serve.

COUNTING CALORIES

For many, including myself, dieting is a way of life. A very successful and clever woman who was New York's top model during the late 1920s gave this advice on the subject in her advanced years and in an advanced state of wisdom: "In order to retain your figure, you must give up eating breakfast on your thirtieth birthday, lunch at forty, and dinner at fifty."

She did not, however, follow her own advice. In her late sixties—still looking as elegant and slim as ever—she ate. Every night. And what do you suppose she dined on? Chicken breast. (Without the skin, of course.) Statistically speaking, a 6½-ounce serving has but 197 calories, with an amazing 74 grams of protein. If there's any doubt in your mind about the perfect diet food, let it be put to rest. It is undoubtedly chicken breast.

VEGETABLE AND PASTA CHICKEN SALAD

6–8 servings

Chicken Breasts

4 cups chicken stock
Salt and black pepper
3 whole chicken breasts (about 3 pounds), halved
½ cup light olive oil
3 teaspoons sherry wine vinegar
1 garlic clove, minced
2 scallions (white and green parts), minced

Vegetables

8 asparagus spears, trimmed, cooked until crisp-tender, and cut into 1-inch lengths
2 cups broccoli florets, cooked until crisp-tender
1 cup green beans, cooked until crisp-tender and cut into ½-inch diagonal pieces
6 scallions (white and some of the green part), chopped
½ cup finely diced sweet red pepper

Vegetable Marinade

⅓ cup olive oil
¼ cup white wine vinegar
2 tablespoons sherry wine vinegar
Salt and black pepper to taste

6 whole large red cabbage leaves
1 bunch large fresh spinach leaves, washed and stems removed
1 pound small tube pasta, such as penne or ziti cooked until *al dente*, rinsed, drained, and chilled
2 scallions (white and green parts), minced
½ pound cherry tomatoes

1. In a large saucepan or stockpot, bring the stock to a boil; stir in the salt and pepper. Add the chicken breasts, arrange in a single layer, and cover. Lower the heat and simmer 8 to 10 minutes, or until firm. Remove from the heat, uncover, and let cool in the stock. Remove the skin and bones. Cut the chicken breasts into bite-size pieces. Transfer to a large bowl and add the oil, vinegar, garlic, and scallions. Toss gently; refrigerate, covered, until you are ready to assemble the salad.

2. Mix the vegetables with the marinade ingredients. Toss, cover, and refrigerate.

3. To prepare the serving platter, ring the outer edge with the large cabbage leaves. In the center, create a bed for the chicken breast mixture using the spinach leaves. At the last minute, toss the pasta and the vegetables together. Place on the platter, leaving a well in the center for the chicken. Place the chicken in the well, sprinkle with scallions, and decorate the platter with cherry tomatoes. Keep refrigerated until serving time.

Mail-Order Guide

Bazaar Français of the Market, Inc.
688 Sixth Ave.
New York, NY 10010
Equipment, excellent selection

Bissinger's
205 West 4th St.
Cincinnati, OH 45202
Equipment and selection of ingredients

Bridge Kitchenware
214 East 52nd St.
New York, NY 10022
Equipment

Dean & DeLuca
121 Prince St.
New York, NY 10012
*Spices, equipment, exotic ingredients, including a
variety of dried mushrooms, and spices and herbs*

Istanbul Express
2432 Durrant Ave.
Berkeley, CA 94704
Excellent selection of exotic spices

The Kobos Company
5531 S.W. Macadam
Portland, OR 97201
Equipment and spices

Levkar by the Barrel
H. Roth and Son
1577 First Ave.
New York, NY 10028
*Excellent selection of equipment and ingredients,
spices*

Maid of Scandinavia
3244 Raleigh Ave.
Minneapolis, MN 55416
Equipment, ingredients and spices

Paprika Weiss Importer
1546 Second Ave.
New York, NY 10028
*Ingredients including spices (whole and ground) and
some equipment*

Williams-Sonoma
Mail Order Department
P.O. Box 7456
San Francisco, CA 94120
*Excellent selection of equipment (including boning
knives), some ingredients and books*

Zabar's
2245 Broadway
New York, NY 10024
Discount equipment and most ingredients

Index